★ ANDREW JACKSON ★

MILTON MELTZER

ANDREW JACKSON

JACKSON

AND HIS AMERICA

FRANKLIN WATTS

NEW YORK ★ CHICAGO ★ LONDON ★ TORONTO ★ SYDNEY

Frontispiece: Andrew Jackson as painted by Thomas Sully around 1824. This image was the model for the Jackson portrait on the twenty-dollar bill.

Maps by Vantage Art
Photographs copyright ©: National Gallery of Art, Washington, DC, Andrew W. Mellon Collection: p. 2; The Bettmann Archive: pp. 14, 17, 35, 50, 56, 98, 105, 116, 154, 190; Ladies Hermitage Association: pp. 25, 81, 147, 149; New York Public Library, Special Collections: pp. 53, 159; New York Public Library, Picture Collection: p. 64; National Archives: p. 68; The Warner Collection of Gulf States Paper Corporation, Tuscaloosa, AL: p. 74; Florida State Archives, Photographic Collection: p. 77; National Portrait Gallery, Smithsonian Institution: p. 97; Library of Congress: pp. 109, 111 top, 111 bottom left, 139, 141, 167, 172; Tennessee State Library and Archives: p. 111 bottom right; City of Boston Arts Commission: p. 120; Woolaroc Museum, Bartlesville, OK: p. 131; The Clements Library, University of Michigan, Ann Arbor: p. 183; National Museum of American Art, Washington, DC/Art Resource, NY: p. 186; International Museum of Photography at George Eastman House: p. 195.

Library of Congress Cataloging-in-Publication Data

Meltzer, Milton, 1915–
Andrew Jackson : and his America / Milton Meltzer.
p.   cm.
Includes bibliographical references and index.
Summary: A look at the life and times of our seventh president.
ISBN 0-531-11157-1
1. Jackson, Andrew, 1767–1845 2. Presidents—United States—Biography. 3. United States—Politics and government—1829–1837. [1. Jackson, Andrew, 1767–1845. 2. Presidents. 3. United States—Politics and government—1829–1837.]
I. Title.
E382.M47   1993
973.5'6'092—dc20
[B]   93-3947 CIP AC

CONTENTS

★ ALSO BY MILTON MELTZER ★

Thomas Jefferson:
The Revolutionary Aristocrat

Columbus and the World Around Him

Benjamin Franklin:
The New American

Mark Twain:
A Writer's Life

The Bill of Rights:
How We Got It and What It Means

The American Revolutionaries:
A History in Their Own Words

Voices from the Civil War

African-American History:
Four Centuries of Black Life
(with Langston Hughes)

American Politics:
How It Really Works

The Black Americans:
A History in Their Own Words

Starting from Home:
A Writer's Beginnings

All Times, All Peoples:
A World History of Slavery

Poverty in America

Crime in America

The Amazing Potato

★ ANDREW JACKSON ★

INTRODUCTION

What can you believe?

Some say that Andrew Jackson, America's seventh president, was mild, amiable, polite, polished, benevolent, and democratic.

Others say he was rude, crude, rash, despotic, tyrannical, and murderous.

They said these things while Jackson was alive, some 150 years ago. And there are historians and biographers who say them now.

What is the truth?

Who was the real Andrew Jackson?

Perhaps he was a mixture of several of these contradictory elements. To find out, it would help mightily if we could put ourselves in the place of someone who lived in Jackson's time. The biographer tries to do that, as best he can. He hopes for success and draws some comfort from the knowledge that Jackson can't appear on the scene to contradict him.

The subject of any biographer has to be imagined in his own time and setting. That is not easy. The America Jackson was born into was still a British colony. And when he died, the new nation was barely fifty years old. The differences between Jackson's day and our own are immense. Yet human personality is essentially the same today as it was then. The forms of expression may differ, but not the motives. What drove Jackson in his time

drives people now. The specific historical circumstances, of course, were unique to his time and need to
be recaptured if we are to understand how Jackson was
shaped by them, used them, surmounted them, or was
overwhelmed by them.

If this biography comes at least within calling distance of Jackson and his world, then it will help us to
discover something about ourselves—as individuals and
as a nation.

1

"I FELT UTTERLY ALONE"

★

Andrew Jackson was born poor and died rich.

He proved that the American dream of log cabin to White House was possible, for he was the first self-made man to become president of the United States.

Andrew—named for his father—was born to one of the many Ulster families driven out of Ireland when the English made life miserable for them. The Jacksons were part of the great influx of non-English immigrants to America in the 1700s—the Irish Protestants, the Scots, and the Germans. Tenant farmers from County Antrim, the Jacksons crossed the North Atlantic in the spring of 1765. Landing in Philadelphia, they made their way down the valley of the Appalachians to settle in the Waxhaw region of the Carolinas. It seemed a good place for Andrew senior, his wife Elizabeth and their two young sons, Hugh and Robert, to start an American life. For here, family and neighbors from home had already put down roots. Ties were close in the backcountry; if anyone rose to fame or fortune, he pulled up family and friends with him.

Andrew senior scratched out a bare living in the poor red clay for two years. He built a small log cabin for his family and managed to feed them decently. Then, just before his wife was to bear their third child, he died suddenly—either from an injury or illness, no one is sure. After his burial, Mrs. Jackson went to the home of her sister and brother-in-law, the Crawfords, in the Lan-

*The log cabin in South Carolina where
Andrew Jackson was born.*

caster district of South Carolina. On March 15, 1767,
she bore her third son, Andrew. It was decided that the
Jacksons would make their permanent home with the
Crawfords.

A small woman with vivid blue eyes and red hair,
Elizabeth Jackson was one of a feisty family of Hutchin-
son sisters. Several had ventured unmarried from
Northern Ireland to marry countrymen on the eastern
seaboard of the colonies and march into the wilderness
with them. Elizabeth took over housekeeping for the
Crawfords, nursed her ailing sister, and tended to her
(Elizabeth's) three little boys.

For about a dozen years, Andrew lived at the Crawfords'. He learned reading, writing, and figuring in local
schools but never got the education of men like John

Adams or Thomas Jefferson. History? He knew nothing about it, and little more of mathematics or the sciences. He showed no interest in literature; it was said he read only one novel from beginning to end. The Bible, yes, at least now and then. It was only the newspapers he paid close attention to.

There was one day's newspaper he would never forget. It arrived in August 1776, many weeks after the great event it reported; it carried the text of the Declaration of Independence. Andy—as everyone called the tall, slim nine-year-old—read every word of it aloud to the less literate neighbors who had come to the house to hear it. "In Congress, July 4, 1776. The Unanimous Declaration of the Thirteen United States of America. When, in the course of human events . . ."

Andy was holding center-stage, and he liked that. He had a great sense of drama, and throughout life he would cast himself in a starring role. One of his earliest biographers said he had the reputation of a "wild, frolicsome, willful, mischievous, daring, reckless boy." Many noted the riveting power of his gaze. When he was angered, his blue eyes blazed, and people quailed under the look. He was dictatorial by temperament and sometimes played the bully. One of his modern biographers, Robert Remini, writes that "Jackson was a fighting cock all his life who was very kind to hens who clucked about him for protection and sustenance; but he would savage with beak and spur any other cock who dared to challenge him or question his word." Looking back over his life, it seems to be the story of one fight after another, some important, some foolish, but all colorful.

From village brawling Andy graduated to real war, the war for independence the Americans were fighting against the British crown. The battles didn't reach his territory till the British invaded South Carolina and seized both Savannah and Charleston. A band of redcoats raided the Waxhaw lands, killing over a hundred people and wounding more. Andy's oldest brother, Hugh, at sixteen had joined an American regiment fighting in South Carolina. At the close of a battle, Hugh died, not of wounds but of heat exhaustion.

Andy himself, although only thirteen, joined up too and served the troops as a mounted messenger. After one of the battles in 1780, both Andy and his brother Robert returned home. Fighting swirled all around the Waxhaws as Patriot and Tory neighbors killed each other in what was a civil war as well as a war against an empire. In one bloody encounter, the two Jackson boys were taken prisoner by British dragoons. A British officer ordered Andy to clean his boots. The boy refused, claiming his right as a prisoner of war not to be treated like a servant. The furious officer whipped out his sword and slashed at the boy's head. Instinctively, Andy flung up his left hand to ward off the blow, but the sword cut deeply into his head and hand, leaving scars he carried all his life. And a hatred for the British, too.

Andy and Robert were jammed into a jail with 250 other captured Patriots. Both boys caught smallpox when the dread disease invaded the prison. Fortunately, their mother arrived to visit them while the British and American commanders were arranging an exchange of prisoners. She got the British to include her sons in the exchange, along with a few other Waxhaw neighbors.

Robert, weakened terribly both by smallpox and an infected wound, had to be tied to his horse for the 40-mile journey home. Through a heavy persistent rain, Andy walked—barefoot, bareheaded, coatless—while his mother rode a pony. Two days after they reached home, Robert was dead and Andy fading rapidly. But his mother wouldn't let her last child's life slip away. With fierce determination, she nursed the boy through a slow recovery that took several months. When his life seemed safe, Mrs. Jackson felt her duty now was to make the 160 mile journey to Charlestown Harbor, to

Young Andrew Jackson defying a British officer during the American Revolution. The legendary incident was depicted much later in a lithograph by Currier & Ives.

help American soldiers lying sick in British prison ships. But while nursing the plague-ridden men, she caught cholera herself and died. She was buried in an unmarked grave in Charleston.

Andy received the news together with a small bundle of his mother's clothing. "I felt utterly alone," he said.

The Revolutionary War came to an end just as Elizabeth Jackson died. Cornwallis surrendered at Yorktown; the new nation now stood on its own. So did young Andrew. Loss of family—parents and brothers, all gone—plunged him into deep melancholy. But the years of growing up amid the clash of arms had toughened him. Proud of his share in the fight for freedom, Andy knew the heavy price paid for victory. As wars often do, it made him passionately patriotic.

Where would he live? A cousin took him in for a while and then passed him on to an uncle. He worked in a saddler's shop and found friends among some upper-class boys from Charleston. Their families had fled the British-occupied city for the Waxhaws. They were a wild lot: nothing interested them but drinking, gambling, cockfighting, and brawling. Andy took to that life happily.

Later, people recalled incidents that suggest what shaped Jackson. When he was twelve, for instance, an eighteen-year-old beat him up badly. Andy's uncle demanded the bully be arrested for assault and battery. "No, Sir!" said Andy's mother. "No son of mine shall ever appear as a complaining witness in a case of assault and battery! If he gets hold of a fellow too big for him, let him wait till he grows some and then try it again!"

His mother's grit became part of Andy. Although he was too skinny to be a good wrestler, he never avoided a match. One of his boyhood friends said, "I could throw him three times out of four, but he never *stayed* throwed. He was dead game and would *never* give up." Once a friend handed him a gun to fire that was loaded to the muzzle. When Andy shot it off, the recoil knocked him to the ground. Instantly, he jumped up and yelled, "By God, if one of you laughs, I'll kill him!"

When the British moved out of Charleston in 1782, Andy's friends returned to their homes, and he followed them. No family was at hand to control him. He went wild, to the despair of relatives who heard of his outrageous doings.

Horses, horses, horses. That was all the talk in the taverns and parlors of Charleston. At race time schools closed, courts of law closed, merchants locked their doors to go off to the track. Andy had earned a reputation as a good judge of horseflesh, but his luck was bad. A small inheritance from his grandfather in Ireland was soon wasted as he gambled it away at the racetrack.

★

Despite his violent temper, Andy was a popular teenager. He loved company, joined in everyone's games, and delighted in dancing. But with nothing left to live on, he gave up Charleston and returned to the Waxhaws, where he went back to school. A year later, he was teaching school himself. One wonders what his pupils learned from him. Then, at the age of seventeen, he turned to the law. Many of the Revolution's leaders had been prosperous lawyers. It was an honored profession, and promised a bright future.

So Andy left the Waxhaws for good, and moved north to Salisbury, a country seat in North Carolina. A prominent attorney, Spruce MaCay, took him on as a sort of apprentice, the customary way to study law in that time. Andy found a room in the town tavern, a hangout for other MaCay law students. Reading the thick, dry law books on the office shelves was heavy going. He learned too by copying documents and legal papers, and to help out with the chores he ran errands and cleaned up the office. He watched how MaCay conducted his practice and listened to his advice.

Those were long and boring days for a restless young man; he had to find some outlet for his explosive energy. At night, when he left the office, he met his friends for fun and frolic. They had felt his magnetic authority at once, and out of respect—or fear—would go wherever he led. Especially on drunken sprees. One of their memorable exploits was the night they partied at a tavern. Toasting one another, they smashed the glasses on the floor and, not content with that, broke up the table, wrecked the chairs, ripped the curtains, and set the junked room ablaze.

All Salisbury quickly pegged Andy as a hell-raiser. The locals remembered him as "the most roaring, rollicking, game-cocking, horse-racing, card-playing, mischievous fellow that ever lived in Salisbury . . . the head of the rowdies hereabouts . . . more in the stable than in the office."

Andy stayed with MaCay for about two years. Then in 1786, he moved over to the office of John Stokes, one of the state's leading lawyers. Six months later, two state judges, after examining the twenty-year-old, admitted him to the bar. For a year he drifted about the state's local courts, taking a case here and there, to little profit. A young woman who liked to visit the court when it sat in Salisbury recorded her impressions of Andrew dressed up in "a new suit, with broadcloth coat and ruffled shirt, his abundant dark red hair combed carefully back, and, I suspect, made to lay down smooth with bear's oil. He was full six feet tall and very slender, but graceful. His eyes were handsome, a kind of steel-blue. I have talked with him a great many times and never saw him avert his eyes from me for an instant."

Andrew was getting nowhere, until John McNairy, one of his old friends at MaCay's, gave him an opening. McNairy had just been made a judge for the Western District of North Carolina, which then stretched as far as the Mississippi River. The wilderness territory included what would become the state of Tennessee. McNairy had the power to appoint the public prosecutor, and Jackson accepted his offer of the new job. It would guarantee him a salary, allow him to continue his law practice, and give him the chance to explore the frontier many people were now heading for.

So in the spring of 1788, Andrew rode across the Allegheny Mountains through 200 miles of Indian country to begin a new life with the settlers of Tennessee. He carried half a dozen law books, two pistols, and a rifle, and trailing behind was his troop of hunting dogs.

2

THE LAWYER TAKES
A WIFE

No sooner did Jackson arrive in Jonesborough, the main town in East Tennessee, than he got himself into a duel. In Jackson's day gentlemen were always eager to demonstrate their honor and their courage. It happened when Jackson came up in court against an experienced lawyer named Avery. When Jackson presented his client's case in the lawsuit, Avery gently teased the novice for the way he clung to the style of an elementary law book. Jackson flew into a rage and challenged the man to a duel. Neither one wanted to die for such a trifle, so friends arranged a deal. When the two men met at sundown, both fired into the air. Honor was restored; they shook hands and parted.

It was the first of many duels to come, some bloody and deadly. It showed how hotheaded Jackson was when he thought his reputation was at stake. Still, he could calculate his chances and act prudently. He knew Avery was a much better shot, and why get himself killed or crippled?

Jackson lingered in Jonesborough for a few months, then, with a band of settlers, the first to use the new Cumberland Road, moved on to Nashville. With him went a female slave of about eighteen whom he had purchased for $200. On the trail the band kept close watch for Indian raiding parties. Late in October of 1788 they entered Nashville. It was nothing but two stores, two taverns, one whiskey distillery, and one courthouse, rimmed by cabins, tents, and wagons.

The courthouse where McNairy and Jackson would administer the law was a ramshackle and filthy building some eighteen feet square. Debtors ran the town, defying the property owners they owed money to. Andrew meant to show them the power of the law. In his first thirty days he enforced seventy writs of execution against the debtors. This is *our* man, said the well-to-do, and they promptly gave the young prosecutor all the private business he could handle. In just one year, he appeared in 206 of the 435 lawsuits in Nashville.

Jackson couldn't help but get rich. Because money was scarce on the frontier and land was abundant, he often took his legal fees in land. And as public prosecutor, he took his pay in the form of deeds to thousands of acres of public land. It was land that had belonged to the Indians, but it had been taken from them largely by force or fraud. Like most of the frontier elite, Jackson speculated in land. Men with money to invest bought up tracts of land as cheaply as possible, taking a chance on prices going up high enough for them to make fat profits. It didn't take Jackson long to acquire huge holdings. The days of log cabin poverty were far behind him while he was still in his twenties.

In those years, Tennessee lawyers rode circuit, moving from court to court together with the sitting judge. Often they roomed together, drank together, ate together. The same lawyers would oppose one another in case after case. Their prestige depended less on their knowledge of the law than on their skill in courtroom oratory.

When Nashville was founded, the settlers included Colonel John Donelson, his wife, and their eleven children. The youngest was a vivacious girl named Rachel. Three years before Jackson arrived, the Donelson clan had moved to Kentucky, where young Rachel had married Lewis Robards. Then Donelson brought his family back to Nashville, leaving Rachel behind with her husband. Soon after, Donelson was found dead in the woods, murdered by someone unknown.

It was at the widow Donelson's that Andrew went to live when he came to Nashville. He shared a cabin with John Overton, who became a close friend. Mrs. Donelson was glad to have young men as boarders because they offered protection against Indian attacks. There Andrew met Rachel Robards. She had returned alone to her family because her jealous and quarrelsome husband made her marriage a nightmare. Rachel was known as "the best story-teller, the best dancer, the sprightliest companion, the most dashing horsewoman in the western country." But Robards couldn't stand the way she attracted men, and he sent her back to Nashville.

Robards soon changed his mind, however, and begged Rachel to take him back. When she gave in, he came to Tennessee, and for a time they stayed with Rachel's mother because the Indians made living too risky for a couple alone. More trouble was brewing, for all the Donelsons, including Rachel, showed a great liking for Andrew. The jealous husband stood in sad contrast to this gallant young lawyer.

Several times that year, Robards went into fits of rage over what he took to be Rachel's flirtatious behavior and Jackson's response. Yet Robards himself was accused of leaving his wife's bed to spend the night with women in the slave quarters.

Jackson decided it was best to move out to protect Rachel's reputation, and he found a room elsewhere. Robards stayed a while longer, then returned to Kentucky. With no reason to restrain their feelings any longer, Andrew and Rachel were soon passionately in love.

In the fall of 1790, Rachel heard a rumor that Robards meant to come back to Nashville and force her to return to Kentucky with him. Panicked, she decided to flee to Natchez, where relatives and friends could keep her safe. The route was dangerous, and any one of the Donelson men could have accompanied her. But strangely, Jackson insisted on going, although he must have known he was opening himself and Rachel to malicious gossip.

Jackson left Rachel in Natchez and returned to Nashville. Word soon came that Robards had got a divorce. (But the story was false. He had only secured permission to bring suit against his wife for divorce.) At once, Jackson hurried back to Natchez to marry Rachel. Returning to Nashville, they began a married life together that would last thirty-seven years, until her death.

But a terrible mistake had been made that would haunt Jackson and hound Rachel to the end. Two years after their marriage, the truth came out: Robards had not received a divorce until 1793. A court granted it to him on the grounds that Rachel had deserted him "to live in adultery with another man."

When the shocking news reached the couple, they realized Rachel had unintentionally committed bigamy. They obtained a license and went through another marriage ceremony on January 18, 1794. Scholars studying the records have raised doubts about the dates and other circumstances of their two marriages. Possibly Jackson and Rachel had begun to live together before formal marriage. In any case, political enemies would later level the charge of adultery against both Rachel and Jackson. It would not be the first—nor the last—time that charges of actual or alleged sexual misbehavior would be raised against presidential candidates.

Jackson made it plain that he would defend his wife's honor to the death. Let any man breathe her name except in honor, and he would be obliged to face Jackson on the dueling ground. Probably, Rachel never got over

*Rachel Donelson Jackson, painted by Ralph E. W. Earl
in 1827, the year before her death.*

the scandal. From a carefree girl defiant of social convention, she turned into a pious woman withdrawn from
public affairs.

Jackson, never one to take a backseat, climbed rapidly into the top bracket on the Cumberland frontier.
Among the Donelson clan he had married into were

some of the richest people in Tennessee. Many of them were highly influential in politics too. As more and more settlers moved west, opportunity for power and wealth expanded. Soon Jackson acquired a large plantation at Hunter's Hill, near Nashville. Rachel was of great help in its management, especially because he was often obliged to be away for long periods. Their love, often expressed in tender letters, grew with the years.

Inevitably, Jackson's life became entangled with both Indians and African Americans. As white settlers advanced into their territory, the Indians resisted. Fights between the two groups were frequent. Almost every week someone—Indian or white—was killed near Nashville. In fact, the whole town of Nashville occupied land in violation of a treaty with the Indians.

Soon after his arrival in Nashville, Jackson had joined a military company sent out to punish Indians who had raided a white settlement. His comrades reported he was "bold, dashing, fearless" and always spoiling for combat with the Indians. His reputation as an Indian fighter had begun. Like most of the whites, he cared nothing for a treaty that respected the rights of Indians. When a treaty guaranteed Indians a piece of territory, the whites would break it and then insist on a new treaty to legalize the violation.

The Indians in this region were the Cherokees. During the American Revolution, they had been allies of the British. With the war over, the United States made a separate peace with the Cherokees. It recognized their independence and established the boundaries of the Cherokee nation, where Indian law was to be supreme. But white settlers were always breaking into their lands. Their contempt for Indian rights so angered President George Washington that he threatened to crush the greedy land speculators by sending in the Army. To prevent that, in 1791 the whites agreed to another treaty (in which the Cherokees gave up still more territory).

The whites broke the treaty at once, with Jackson as guilty as the others.

Enraged, the Indians began to attack settlements in their territory, even threatening the capital at Knoxville. Going out to scout the movements of the Indians, Jackson narrowly escaped death while a friend accompanying him was killed.

Jackson never could put himself in the place of the Indians. In this he was much like the other white settlers. They saw the fields and forests of America as rightfully *their* domain, to develop, to exploit, to control as they wished. Many felt they had a divine mission to spread white civilization over this new land. The Indians, who had lived here for tens of thousands of years, were only an obstacle to their drive for possession. And Jackson was as bloody-minded in his desire to remove the Indians as the worst of the whites.

On this issue of Indian removal, Jackson demanded that the central government take a strong hand. Yet if it appeared that government would take action to curtail property rights or slavery, he took the opposite view. The only principle—if you could call it that—underlying his stance on government was self-interest. Whatever suited his needs was right; otherwise, it was wrong.

By now Tennesseans were ready to claim statehood in the young and growing Union. In 1796, Jackson was one of the delegates chosen to write a constitution for Tennessee as a step toward that goal. Although he would build his political reputation as spokesman for the rights of the common man, already he was setting limits to those rights. He did support simple residency for all free men as the sole condition for voting. But to be elected to the legislature a candidate had to own at least 200 acres. And to be chosen governor, he must own 500 acres.

During the constitutional debates, Jackson displayed his famous wild temper and superpatriotic passion. He yelled at any who crossed him, threatened violence, demanded extreme action. And always he stood for states' rights. To him and his fellow frontiersmen, the state was all-important, not the federal government. (Yet years later, in 1830, he took the opposite view.) The national government way off in Philadelphia was remote from their everyday needs. Let it keep out of their way. They had made their own life in the West and counted on no one else for help. (Except to get rid of the Indians.)

In June 1796, Tennessee became the sixteenth state in the Union. One of the two senators elected to represent the state was its political boss, William Blount, a land speculator born without a hint of morality in his blood. Without his political blessing it was impossible to advance in Tennessee. It was Blount who had appointed the ambitious young Andrew as attorney general and then as judge advocate of a military regiment. Now Blount decided that Jackson was the man to run for Tennessee's single seat in the U.S. House of Representatives. He had ample evidence of Jackson's loyalty and could count on him to defend the frontier in its running fight with the Indians and to carry out whatever else the party asked of him. The Blount machine and Andrew's popularity won the seat easily. In the late fall of 1796, at the age of twenty-nine, Jackson arrived in Philadelphia to serve as Tennessee's first congressman.

3

THE HABIT
OF DOMINATION
★

So here we have Andrew Jackson, not yet thirty, taking his first step on the national stage. The year is 1796. George Washington, just completing his second term in the presidency, has given the nation his Farewell Address. After a fierce fight between John Adams and Thomas Jefferson for the highest office, the Federalists have barely elected Adams, and Jefferson has become vice president. Jefferson's party (then called the Republicans, but actually the forerunner of what is now the Democratic Party) has been growing stronger, and threatens soon to replace the Federalists in power.

What was the United States like when Jackson began his climb to the top?

A few facts will point up the immense gap between then and now. Today our population is about 250 million. Then, 200 years ago, it was only 4 million, or about the number of people living in Detroit today. Philadelphia, with 42,000 people, was the biggest city, and New York was second with 33,000. The most populous state was Virginia, with some 800,000 people.

The population of the nation was split fifty-fifty between north and south. Most people (two-thirds of them) lived within fifty miles of the Atlantic. The region beyond, where Jackson had settled, was still only thinly settled with whites.

It was a time of great promise for the new nation. It was starting an experiment in national republican government no one before had attempted. The people, land, and natural resources needed to make the experiment a success seemed unlimited.

In the North, great changes in the economic system were on the horizon. Improvements in transportation and manufacturing came on rapidly. As production became bigger and more mechanized, skilled craftsmen began to see the nature of their work change. In New England, capitalists would bring workers together to make products in the nation's first factories. Family farming still dominated food production, but some young people would begin to leave home to work in the new enterprises of the cities.

A network of new roads and canals spread from place to place, taking consumer goods from the Northeast to new settlements in the Midwest and carrying back raw material and foodstuffs needed in the East.

The pace of change was much slower in the South, where little was being done to increase manufacturing or improve transportation. Cotton would rapidly replace tobacco as the South's major cash crop. A plantation economy built on the labor of enslaved African Americans would spread from the states of the South's upper region into the deep South.

The institution of slavery would dominate political life for a long time to come. Jackson grew up in the Waxhaws at a time when slave traders from the coast paraded their wares up the post road and auctioned them off at Charlotte. These consisted of black men, women, and children who had just been removed from the holds of the slave ships that plied the Middle Passage between the African and American continents.

By 1790, when he was twenty-one, the young lawyer was adding to his income by buying and selling slaves. When a friend needed a loan, Jackson advanced the money in return for the promise of early repayment with "a likely country-born Negro boy or girl." In the same year, he took charge of a runaway slave who had fled from New Orleans and returned the slave to his owner.

Over the years, Jackson would accumulate many slaves. By 1794 he owned 10; in 1798 it was 15; in 1820, 44; and by the time he was elected president it was 95. Soon after, the number climbed to 150, making Jackson one of the largest Tennessee planters.

Was he a cruel slave master? Like most big planters of his time, he was concerned about the health of his slaves. They were property, investments crucial for business success and social standing. He exercised his right to buy and sell them to make a profit. He even bet them on horse races. If slaves broke his rules, he had them whipped and sometimes chained. Jackson had no mercy for slaves who tried to escape bondage. In 1804 he advertised for a runaway in a Nashville newspaper, promising a fifty-dollar reward and "ten dollars extra, for any hundred lashes any person will give him, to the amount of three hundred."

The habit of domination, of insisting upon imposing his will upon all others, came early and easily to Jackson. We saw it expressed in youth. The system of slavery required total power from the owner, total submission from the slave, even though kindly paternalism might tinge relationships between this master and that slave. But masters often took pleasure in the exercise of sadistic domination, as evidenced in Jackson's offer of a bonus if a runaway was given an extra beating.

It was about this time that Thomas Jefferson, in his book *Notes on Virginia*, confessed how troubled he was about the damaging effects of bondage upon master as well as slave. He wrote:

There must doubtless be an unhappy influence on the manners of our people produced by the existence of slavery among us. The whole commerce between master and slave is a perpetual exercise of the most boisterous passions, the most unremitting despotism on the one part, and degrading submission on the other. Our children see this and learn from it. . . . The parent storms, the child looks on, catches the lineaments of wrath, puts on the same airs in the circle of smaller slaves, gives a loose to the worst of passions, and thus nursed, educated, and daily exercised in tyranny, cannot but be stamped by it with odious peculiarities. The man must be a prodigy who can retain his manners and morals undepraved by such circumstances. . . .

If a Jefferson was not immune to this influence, certainly Jackson was not. In his rise to power, along both military and political routes, Jackson would prove how authoritarian was his style of leadership, and how indifferent he could be to the welfare of whole categories of people—black or red—for whom he had only contempt.

The first day Jackson took his seat in Congress, his appearance was noted by Albert Gallatin, a leader of the House: "Tall, lanky, uncouth-looking personage with long locks of hair hanging over his face, and a cue down his back tied in an eel-skin . . . his dress singular—manners those of a rough backwoodsman." Early business was a vote on a resolution paying tribute to the retiring President Washington for his services to the nation. Jackson was one of a dozen who voted against it; he didn't like Washington's policy on the Indians. Among the few other actions he took was to get Tennessee reimbursed for the expenses of its campaign against the Cherokees, to win a U.S. marshal's job for his brother-in-law, and to call for a bigger navy.

As his first and only term ended, he wrote Rachel:

My Dearest Heart—

With what pleasing hopes I view the future when I shall be restored to your arms there to spend my days with you the Dear Companion of my life, never to be separated from you again. . . . I mean to retire from public life. . . .

At this stage, Jackson showed little political ambition. He accepted appointment or elective offices more because they added to his social standing, and he gave them up readily. He was home only a few months, however, when one of Tennessee's seats in the U.S. Senate fell vacant and he was asked to fill it. So in September 1797 he was back in the capital to enter the upper house in more elegant style—a black coat with velvet collar, fitted by his Philadelphia tailor. He did nothing to distinguish himself in serving for the next several months. He did make an impression on Thomas Jefferson, who as vice president was presiding over the Senate. Later, Jefferson recalled that Jackson "could never speak on account of the rashness of his feelings. I have seen him attempt it repeatedly, and as often choke with rage. . . . He is a dangerous man." In April 1798 Jackson returned home and resigned his Senate seat. "He had assumed responsibilities far beyond his reach," wrote his biographer Robert V. Remini, "and he virtually made a fool of himself."

Jackson found business at his plantation had gone well. He bought one of the newfangled cotton gins developed by Eli Whitney, finding that it did the work it once took forty slaves to do. He added a profitable whiskey distillery, selling the product at a new merchandising operation he opened in partnership with a friend. Then, just at the close of 1798, his political cronies had him elected by the legislature to the Tennessee Superior Court, the highest court of the state.

He much preferred this post to the U.S. Senate seat, for it would keep him close to Rachel, yet get him around the state enough to enlarge his circle of political contacts. He was no legal scholar, but his way of making swift and simple decisions pleased the people. "Do what is right," he would tell juries; "that is what the law always means."

Many stories spread about Judge Jackson that illustrate his temperament. Once, in a village, the local bully, Russell Bean, was brought into court for cutting off the ears of his baby while on a drunken spree. Bean stomped around the court, cursing judge and jury and crowd, and then stomped out the door. Jackson ordered the sheriff to arrest Bean for contempt of court and haul him back inside. Mustering some deputies, the nervous sheriff went after Bean but returned empty-handed, announcing Bean had threatened to "shoot the first skunk that comes within ten feet." Jackson rose from the bench, stormed outdoors, and marched up to Bean, a pistol in each hand. "Now," he roared, "surrender, you infernal villain, this very minute, or I'll blow you through!"

Bean stared into Jackson's blazing eyes, then quietly dropped his gun and said, "It's no use, Judge, I give in." Explaining why to his pals, Bean said, "I looked Jackson in the eye, and I saw shoot, and so I says to myself, it's about time to sing small, and I did."

Judicial records were not kept during Jackson's years on the bench: It is hard to judge his work from other documents. But the popular impression was that he did a good job, and was fearless, honest, stern, and usually just.

Successful as he was on the bench, Jackson strove for still another honor and more power. He had wanted for years to become major general of the Tennessee militia. Officers on the various levels were elected from

Judge Jackson arresting the village bully, Russell Bean.

the ranks below, with the commander in chief chosen by the brigadier generals. In Jackson's earlier try for the post, the governor, John Sevier, had used his influence to kill Jackson's chances. Now, in 1802, when the major general died, the post was once more open. Sevier himself, a three-time governor ineligible to succeed himself, announced his own candidacy. A Revolutionary War hero, he was furious when this upstart, Judge Jackson, a man with trifling military experience, challenged him for the position. The election produced a tie vote, putting the final decision in the hands of Sevier's successor, Governor Roane. A good friend of Jackson's, he broke the tie in his favor. In 1803, at the age of thirty-five, Jackson added to his titles: major general of the Tennessee militia.

He did not parade his military honors—not yet. He preferred to be called "Judge" except when he commanded the militia at mustering time. His troubles with Sevier were by no means over. Sevier, eligible once more, ran again for governor, against Jackson's friend Roane. To help out, Jackson wrote an article exposing Sevier's connection with a land-fraud scheme. Leaning on his popularity as the legendary old soldier, Sevier posed as the persecuted friend of the poor and denied the charge of being a swindler.

Violence was in the air when Jackson and Sevier met by chance in the crowded public square at Knoxville in October 1803. Sevier denounced Jackson for daring to insult a man who had done so much for the people. Jackson replied by citing his own many public services. "Service?" Sevier laughed. "I know of no great service you have rendered the country, except taking a trip to Natchez with another man's wife!"

Jackson exploded. "Great God!" he screamed. "Do you dare mention *her* sacred name?"

"Draw!" roared Sevier, and the crowd scattered as Sevier with a sword and Jackson with a cane went at each other. Shots rang out in the square, but the two men were separated by their friends.

Jackson sent Sevier a challenge to a duel. For ten days charges and countercharges flew back and forth until the two men, accompanied by armed friends, met at a dueling ground outside Knoxville. Each man drew pistols, but took to cursing instead of shooting. After letting off steam, they put their guns away, and both parties rode peaceably back to Knoxville. Sevier won the election. The men never became friends, but their encounter signaled the beginning of intense political rivalry between eastern Tennessee, headed by Sevier, and the west, led by Jackson.

4

"I INTENDED TO KILL HIM"

★

Jackson reached for another high post when President Jefferson, in 1803, bought Louisiana from France. Jackson used all his political pull to be appointed governor of Louisiana. In these last years on the bench, Jackson had got into financial trouble, with debts piling higher and higher. The governorship of the vast new territory would ease his problems considerably. But Jefferson passed him by and gave the office to another man, William Claiborne. His disappointment soured Jackson on Jefferson permanently.

Soon after losing the Louisiana post, Jackson quit his judgeship. He needed to take firm hold of his business affairs if he was to avoid bankruptcy. He sold his plantation at Hunter's Hill and bought 420 acres some ten miles from Nashville, a place he called the Hermitage. At first he and Rachel lived in a simple blockhouse, with one big room downstairs, two rooms above, and a detached kitchen. Only later did he build the elegant manor house that is now a national museum.

Instead of taking up his law practice again—something he never returned to—he enlarged his merchandising operation. In partnership with two men, Jackson opened a cotton gin and distillery and operated three stores in nearby towns. They dealt in rifles, skillets, salt, coffee, port, calico, cotton, tobacco, pelts, and slaves.

★

His farm, meanwhile, was cultivated by slaves under Rachel's management. The slaves raised several crops, with cotton, corn, and wheat bringing in the highest profits. Jackson also bred horses, cows, and mules. He bought a two-thirds interest in a nearby race course, and enlarged it, also adding a tavern and booths for hucksters. His youthful love of racing persisted; he was always looking for improved breeding horses. On one trip he bought a bay stallion named Truxton, trained it himself, and matched it against a horse called Greyhound for a side bet of $5,000—a huge sum for those days. How he raised the money, no one knows. Luckily, Truxton won the famous match. This eased Jackson's money problems and established his reputation as one of the leading turfmen in the West.

The blockhouse near Nashville, Tennessee, where the Jacksons lived in the early 1800s. Rebuilt several times, the house later became the elegant Hermitage, now a national museum.

At the same time, Jackson enlarged his reputation for readiness to resort to violence. In a dispute over the facts about another racing bet in 1806 (the details are too complex to go into here), Jackson confronted a wealthy young Nashville dandy, Charles Dickinson. After many charges and countercharges, Dickinson published a statement in the local paper calling Jackson "a worthless scoundrel . . . a poltroon and a coward." Jackson promptly challenged him to a duel. The two men met across the Kentucky line, and eight paces, or twenty-four feet, were measured off. "Are you ready?" asked a second. Each man replied that he was, and then came the call to "Fire!"

Dickinson—reputed to be the best shot in Tennessee—raised his pistol quickly and fired. The bullet hit Jackson in the chest. He raised his left arm and held it against his chest, standing very still, his teeth clenched. "Great God! Have I missed him?" Dickinson cried out. "Back to the mark!" shouted Jackson's second. Dickinson stood his ground as Jackson raised his pistol slowly and squeezed the trigger. But the hammer stopped at half cock. Jackson could have refused to shoot then, or fired into the air. But he raised his pistol again, aimed, and fired. The bullet passed clean through Dickinson's body, leaving a gaping hole. The man bled to death.

Jackson was led away, blood soaking down his body into his shoes. Dickinson's bullet had shattered two of his ribs and buried itself deep in his chest. Probably the loose-fitting coat he was wearing had saved his life. The wound never healed properly and, for the forty years more he would live, never ceased to trouble him.

Nashville was horrified by what Jackson had done—cold-bloodedly killing a defenseless man. "I intended to kill him," Jackson said; "I would have stood up long enough to kill him if he had put a bullet through my brain."

Jackson regarded dueling as the only defense against slander. He believed the slanderer was worse than the murderer. "The murderer only takes a man's life, he said, "while the slanderer takes away his good reputation and leaves him a living monument to his children's disgrace."

Dueling was common in Jackson's America. It was especially popular in the South. It was at the heart of a "code of honor" which held men accountable for their conduct in a society without stable standards of behavior. Jackson grew up in a frontier marked by fighting, boasting, short tempers, and violent defense of what a man considered his rights. Although personal quarrels can occur anywhere, Americans of that era were incredibly ready to mutilate one another for the slightest cause. For opening a coach window, a Kentuckian came close to killing another man. Not only did Americans fight for silly reasons; they used shocking forms of hurting one another. Stabbing, shooting, gouging out the eye, biting off the nose or ear were all common forms of violence.

As a man who entered life without a distinguished family behind him, Jackson was very touchy about his reputation. "My reputation is dearer to me than life," he told a friend. "The opprobrium that has been attached to my character upon false evidence must be publicly washed away." As Jefferson noted, Jackson could fly into rages so fierce that he stammered and stuttered and was unable to speak coherently.

One of Jackson's early biographers, William Graham Sumner, called such behavior a caricature of the manners of men who swaggered about the courts of England and France a century before Jackson. As for Jackson himself, Sumner had this to say:

He proved himself a quarrelsome man. Instead of making peace he exhausted all the chances of conflict which offered themselves. He was remarkably genial and gentle when things went to suit him, and when he was satisfied with his companions. He was very chivalrous about taking up the cause of any one who was unjustly treated and was dependent. Yet he was combative, and pugnacious, and over-ready to adjust himself for a hostile collision whenever there was any real or fancied occasion. The society in which he lived developed, by its fashions, some of his natural faults.

What was the spirit of that society in which Jackson's "natural faults" developed? "Business is the very soul of an American," wrote Francis Grund; "he pursues it not as a means of procuring for himself and his family the necessary comforts of life, but as the foundation of all human felicity." In town and country, in all classes, the chase for the dollar began in childhood and continued "till the very hour of death."

Thomas Low Nichols, one of Jackson's contemporaries, said that farmers and businessmen pressed themselves to work endlessly. Charles Dickens, who toured America in 1842, found this life of all-work-and-no-play made Americans "such deadly leaden people." Yes, agreed Nichols. Despite years of peace and plenty, we are "not happy. In no country are the faces of the people furrowed with heavier lines of care. . . . Work and worry eat out the hearts of the people and they die before their time." Many such witnesses agreed that Americans had "unlearned to play, to reflect, to rest." All their purposes were immediately focused on one subject: the almighty dollar.

Jackson himself, early on, was driven by that great desire for gain, "the everlasting struggle for wealth," the "giddy passion of money-getting." Nichols concluded that "money is the habitual measure of all things." (How different is it today?)

The notion that in America opportunity was open to

all, and that every citizen was personally responsible for what becomes of himself, was deep-rooted. A European visitor commented that "A man in America is not despised for being poor at the outset . . . but every year which passes, without adding to his prosperity, is a reproach to his understanding or industry."

Imagine, then, how intense the spirit of competition was. People struggled to do better than their neighbors. The business cycle, which brought boom followed always by bust, created a vast number of failures. Careers zigzagged wildly, with disastrous failures commonplace.

Land was, of course, the most abundant resource in Jackson's day. It was important for farming, for real estate dealing, and as a springboard into a new community. Jackson was gripped by the same land hunger that pervaded all classes of society. He too was a reckless speculator in land—even while in the White House—and like so many other seemingly respectable people was ready to clinch deals on either side of the law.

In the next few years, Jackson went on buying and selling land and slaves at a high profit, and finding good markets for his crops of cotton. His racing stable earned him more than $20,000 in prize money, and the stud fees for his stallions added to his wealth. He enjoyed the high life of the successful planter, making his house the center of hospitality for family, friends, and even strangers who came by. He took great pleasure in his leadership of the state militia. "My pride," he said, "is that my soldiers have confidence in me, and in the event of a war I will lead them on, to victory and conquest."

A sad aspect of Jackson's marriage with Rachel was their inability to have the children they so much wanted. They filled the gap in family life by acting often as guardians for the children of friends or relatives whose fathers had died. Two boys in particular, Andrew Jackson Donelson and Andrew Jackson Hutchings, were especially close wards. Finally, in 1809, the Jacksons legally adopted the newborn son of one of Rachel's relatives, who was too ill to care for the baby herself. They christened him Andrew Jackson, Jr.

It was the War of 1812—America's second war with Britain—which gave Jackson the arena that turned his faults into virtues. The imperious force of his will and the violence of his emotions found an outlet in military combat. War too would give play to an executive talent far beyond what his peacetime pursuits had offered.

There were many causes for that war. For years Britain had seized American ships, kidnapped thousands of American sailors, interfered with American trade, and urged Indians to attack American settlements along the frontier. One of the strongest forces behind the war was psychological: American resentment against Britain's continued attempt to dominate the nation that had broken away from her. Another and far more practical reason was the desire of the Americans to expand their power into Canada, into Florida, and into Indian territory.

Both sides saw the Indian as the key to dominion in the wilderness. Each had long tried to exert influence among the tribes. The whites, as someone pointed out, were "ready to fight to the last Indian" to gain their goals.

Unfortunately, tribes fought against each other, making it easier for the white powers to play on that enmity. Like any other people, the Native Americans had the usual human grievances against their neighbors. The whites were happy to take advantage of those rivalries and of Indian skills in wilderness warfare when it suited their ends.

When Congress met in 1811, a group of newly elected young firebrands from the South and West clamored for war. No more cautious diplomacy, cried the War Hawks, led by Henry Clay of Kentucky and John C. Calhoun of South Carolina. Let's teach Britain a lesson.

Not that they cared about the problems of the merchants and shippers of the East. What they wanted was access to the abundant lands of the West. But the way west was blocked by Indians who refused to be pushed out. The frontier people said it was only because the British in Canada and the Spanish in Florida were stirring up the Indians. The truth they ignored was that the Indians had plenty of reason to resist white invasion.

One of their leaders, the Shawnee chief Tecumseh, appealed for an Indian alliance against the white intruders:

> *The way, and the only way, to check and to stop this evil, is for all the Redmen to unite in claiming a common and equal right to the land, as it was at first and should be yet; for it was never divided, but belongs to all for the use of each.*

No Indians, said Tecumseh, have a right to sell off their common lands, not even to one another. And much less to the whites, who want everything and "will not do with less."

Tecumseh succeeded in building an alliance of Indians pledged to sell no more land and to fight to keep the white people out. This scared settlers on the frontier, and they appealed for help from the governor of Indiana Territory, William Henry Harrison. They had a friend in Harrison, for his sharp practices had cheated the Indians out of most of Indiana for a few dollars. When Harrison learned Tecumseh had gone south to persuade the Creeks, the Cherokees, and the Choctaws to join his confederacy, Harrison led a force of 900 troops to the Tippecanoe River, close to Tecumseh's village. In a brief battle on November 7, 1811, the whites defeated the Indians and burned their village. It broke the power of Tecumseh and the Indians of the old Northwest.

Meanwhile, the War Hawks and President James Madison got ready for war. The president ordered a secret operation to seize West Florida from the Spaniards. A coup was organized, after which the plotters asked for the United States to annex the territory. The president's excuse for doing it was that seizing West Florida was necessary to keep the British from grabbing it first. So the area formally became part of the United States in 1811. When a similar operation was tried in East Florida, the secret agents messed up the scheme.

Months before war would be declared, Jackson took it upon himself to issue a printed call for "Volunteers to arms!" War was on the point of breaking out, he proclaimed. "Shall we, who have clamored for war, now skulk into a corner? . . . No—we are the freeborn sons of the only republic now existing in the world!" The period of youth, he concluded, "is the season for martial exploits." And he signed his call, "Andrew Jackson, Major General."

On June 1, 1812, Madison sent a war message to Congress. He blamed the British for kidnapping American sailors, for issuing orders that allowed the British to plunder American shipping, and for inciting the Indians in the West. Congress voted for war, and American merchants along the coast happily grew rich smuggling and supplying British forces.

Only two weeks after the declaration, the U.S. heard the stunning news that, because of internal pressures and problems, the British had revoked the orders the American blamed them for. But the American desire to seize this chance to conquer Canada was irresistible, and Madison refused to change his policy.

When news that war had begun reached Jackson in Tennessee a few days later, he was delighted. At once he offered the president his militia of 2,500 trained men, promising to move them quickly up to Quebec to conquer Canada. But no word came for him to march on that or any other front. As the months passed without action by his militia, their morale deteriorated. Like their commander, they were spoiling for a fight.

While Jackson waited, everything went wrong on the Canadian front. The invasion ended in utter failure. The Canadians, joined by many Loyalists who had left the United States during the Revolution, imposed a series of humiliating defeats on the Americans. Apparently America had no general who knew how to fight. Except me, thought Jackson, fuming at home.

When the War Department finally acted, it was to order some of the Tennessee militia to join other forces in occupying West Florida. Nothing was said about a role for Jackson. Now forty-five, already old by his day's standards, he begged Tennessee's governor to let him serve, even if only as a sergeant. Why had Washington failed to make use of his friend Jackson? the governor wondered. Finally, the governor signed a federal commission making Jackson a major general of U.S. volunteers. In December, with two infantry regiments under his command, General Jackson glided down the Mississippi in flatboats to Natchez. There he was ordered to stand by on the alert for the moment when his troops would be needed to strike at Pensacola, Mobile, or New Orleans.

For weeks nothing happened. Then the secretary of war ordered Jackson to dismiss his troops and return home. Jackson was furious. How could he dismiss an army of over 2,000 men—without pay, transportation, or medicine—and let them wander home alone through Indian territory! He refused to obey the order. He would march his volunteers the 500 miles back to Nashville.

It took a month for the army to reach Tennessee. Hundreds fell sick along the way, and Jackson and his officers gave up their horses to carry them. Jackson walked alongside his mare, comforted the sick, encouraged the weary, doled out the rations, kept everyone going. His men said the old man was as tough as hickory, and that affectionate nickname—Old Hickory—clung to him forever.

That futile mission turned out to be a personal triumph for Jackson. The powerful will, the great self-confidence, the courage and fortitude that had always been his now shone brilliantly in full public view. His men adored the general, and the legend created on that return home made them eager to follow him anywhere. They knew he was capable of superhuman effort to achieve his will. It was his absolute determination to win at all costs—and not any great military talent—that would account for the victories to come.

5

"WE SHOT THEM LIKE DOGS"

Soon after the volunteers returned to Nashville, Jackson found himself in another scrape that ended in bloodshed. Two of his militia, William Carroll and Jesse Benton, brother of Thomas Hart Benton, a friend of Jackson's, quarreled. When Carroll asked Jackson to be his second, he said he was too old for that now and urged the young men to settle their differences peaceably. That failing, he agreed to second Carroll. The duelists met early one morning in June 1813. At the signal to fire, Benton squatted down to present the smallest target and fired quickly, hitting Carroll in the thumb. When Carroll fired, his bullet raked both buttocks of the squatting Benton. The outcome made Jesse a laughingstock. Thomas Benton, angered by his brother's humiliation, accused Jackson in a letter of conducting the duel in a "savage, unequal, unfair and base manner," and added that a man of Jackson's age and prestige had no business "to conduct a duel about nothing between young men who had no harm against each."

What Benton wrote was widely spread about Nashville, and Jackson threatened to horsewhip Thomas the next time he saw him, for insulting him. Jackson's chance came when he ran into both Bentons in front of a Nashville hotel. Jackson called on Thomas to defend himself and then drew a gun, backing Benton into the hotel. Jesse meanwhile had raised his pistol too, and now he fired at Jackson, hitting him in the arm and shoulder. As Jackson fell forward, he exchanged shots with Thomas, both men missing. Several of Jackson's friends rushed in, and one of them stabbed Jesse in both arms. When Thomas fell backwards down a flight of stairs, the shooting ended.

Jackson's shoulder was shattered by one bullet, and his upper left arm pierced by another. He was carried to a bed in the hotel, bleeding so heavily it soaked through two mattresses. Several doctors came in to work on his wounds, urging him to let them amputate the shattered arm. "I'll keep my arm!" he said as he faded into unconsciousness. They put poultices on the wounds but did not try to remove the slugs. Jackson was unable to leave the bed for three weeks. Not for another twenty years did a surgeon remove the bullets.

Jackson's friends threatened to even the score with the Bentons. "I am literally in hell here," wrote Thomas. He returned to his home in Franklin and quit the Army. Many years later, the two men were reconciled and became political allies. Benton used to say, "I had a fight with Jackson. A fellow was hardly in fashion who didn't."

While Jackson was recuperating from his wounds at the Hermitage, word came that on August 30, Creek Indians had massacred white settlers at Fort Mims in Alabama. The Indian attack had been led by Red Eagle, head of the militant Red Sticks (so named for their bright-red war clubs), who were a faction of the Creek Nation. (The Creeks got that name from the whites because they lived along the rivers and streams in Georgia and Alabama.) Red Eagle was a follower of Tecumseh, the Shawnee who was working to unite the Northern and Southern tribes into a power that could drive out the white settlers. Some of the Lower Creek leaders refused to support Tecumseh's war policy. Together with Cherokee, Choctaw, and Chickasaw warriors, they favored accommodating the U.S. power.

*The assault of the Creek Indians on Fort Mims in 1813,
painted by Alonzo Chappel. Artistic depictions of Indians
as ruthless savages were widely distributed during the
1870s, intensifying the racism that fueled the wars against
the Indian nations following the Civil War.*

Perhaps the whites would be more lenient in return for
the alliance? The result was to turn the Creek War into a
civil war.

Red Eagle with about a thousand Creeks had lain
hidden in the swamps outside Fort Mims till they heard
drums summoning the soldiers to lunch. Then, finding

the fort's gate open, they rushed through and fell upon the soldiers, the settlers, and their families. They killed over 250 people, including women and children. Tennessee's governor summoned 5,000 volunteers and asked Jackson to lead them in repelling the "approaching invasion."

Still very weak from his wounds, Jackson saw this as his chance to win military glory. Crying out that he would avenge the whites on the Alabama frontier, he got out of bed and took command of his troops. A force of Choctaw Indians joined him, for they and the Creeks were traditional enemies. As the Creeks fled from the invaders, Jackson sacked their settlements and burned them down. In one place, near present-day Gadsden, Jackson's men surprised the Creeks at sunrise and killed 186 warriors, then mowed down their women and children. David Crockett said afterwards, "We shot them like dogs."

As Jackson's victories multiplied, many hostile Indian villages switched to his side. In November, Jackson led his troops into Fort Strother, hoping to find desperately needed supplies, long promised, but still not delivered from Nashville. But now he was confronted with mutiny. The volunteers and draftees had had enough; they wanted to go home. Field officers urged Jackson to let the army return to Tennessee. He refused, but the volunteers ignored him and started to march out. Jackson mustered his loyal troops and forced the rebels back into camp. But the rebellion grew worse. A whole brigade made ready to march back to Tennessee, threatening to shoot down anyone who tried to stop them. Grabbing his rifle, Jackson mounted his horse and rode up to face the mutineers. Resting the rifle on his horse's neck (his left arm was still useless), he roared, "I'll shoot dead the first man who makes a move!" No one moved. Minutes passed, then slowly first one man, then another and another and finally whole companies shifted behind their general to block the road home. The mutiny was over; Jackson had added another chapter to the growing legend.

His troubles, however, were by no means ended. On December 10, 1813, the one-year enlistment of the volunteers would be over. They made no secret of their intention to quit on that day. Harsh army discipline, hunger, endless strain, constant fear of surprise attack had made them sick of this life. But Jackson told them no one could leave. In his view, a year's enlistment meant 365 days of active service. But the men counted as part of that year the months they had spent at home while on call from the state. Determined to hold them, Jackson posted his artillery companies in front of and behind the troops who meant to leave. Then he pleaded with them not to desert, promising he'd let them go as soon as the expected reinforcements arrived. Getting no response, he ordered the artillery gunners to prepare to fire the field pieces trained on the mutineers.

The soldiers knew that light in Jackson's eyes: he would shoot if he said he would. They broke ranks and pledged to remain in the fort until new troops would arrive. In a few days the replacements came in, but they too were near the end of their enlistment period, and they soon followed the others home. Jackson was now almost alone, with only one regiment remaining and the Red Sticks but a few miles away.

Disaster was avoided at the last minute. Tennessee had already mustered more troops, and soon Jackson had some 5,000 men at Fort Strother. He quickly began a rigid regime of training to enforce the discipline needed for combat. It was now that his steely will imposed an order that would darken his reputation for the rest of his life. When an eighteen-year-old volunteer, John Woods, got into some minor trouble with an officer, his arrest was ordered. The youngster's temper flared, and he threatened to shoot anyone who dared touch him.

*Adding to the growing legend of the ruthless military
leader was this depiction of General Jackson quelling a
mutiny of his troops during the Creek War. The engraving
is taken from Amos Kendall's biography of Jackson,
published during the 1828 presidential campaign.*

Told a "mutiny" was breaking out, Jackson rushed
from his tent yelling, "Where is the damned rascal?
Shoot him! Blow twenty holes through him!" Woods
meanwhile had already given up his gun and submitted to
arrest. But Jackson would not let the matter drop. He
meant to demonstrate that mutiny wouldn't be tolerated.
A court-martial found Woods guilty and ordered the
young man's execution. Jackson refused to hear pleas for
clemency and had a firing squad execute Woods in front
of the entire army.

The incident deepened the conviction of many that Jackson was a ruthless killer lacking all compassion. He had chosen to kill a young man rather than impose a lighter sentence. That winter's experience of mutinous troops had hardened, if possible, an already icy will. Jackson would show again and again that he would do anything to destroy whatever and whomever he considered an enemy.

The winter of 1813–14 passed with Jackson hunting Red Eagle and his Red Sticks and destroying Creek towns in his path. At the Horseshoe Bend of the Tallapoosa River, the Red Sticks had built a log fortress and awaited Jackson's attack. The Bend was a wooded peninsula surrounded almost completely by water. On the morning of March 27, 1814, Jackson deployed 2,000 troops around the Bend to cut off routes of escape, then brought up his artillery to bombard the log breastwork as his men peppered the Red Sticks with rifle fire.

Meanwhile, other soldiers crossed the river to set fire to huts in the rear of the fort. At the sight of the smoke rising, Jackson ordered an assault upon the breastwork. Fierce fighting held up the charge, but the breastwork was soon breached and the troops rushed into the fort. The Red Sticks backed off into the thick brush and the trees, but the attackers were relentless. "The carnage was dreadful," as Jackson reported later. Many Indians died by knife or bullet while others ran for shelter along the cliffs or jumped down into the river. As the Creeks tried to swim away, Jackson's men shoved their heads under the water and drowned them. For hours the deadly chase continued until the soldiers had slaughtered every warrior they could reach. Only a handful of Red Sticks escaped across the river.

The next day Jackson's men counted 900 dead Red Sticks; 300 were taken prisoner, most of them women and children. Jackson's casualties were 70 killed and 206 wounded. Red Eagle himself, to Jackson's great disappointment, was not at the Bend the day of the battle. The crushing defeat marked the end of Red Stick power. They could no longer war effectively against the United States.

After burying the dead and giving his troops a short rest, Jackson moved on, destroying Indian villages on his way to an old French fort which was now renamed Fort Jackson. With further resistance hopeless, Creek chiefs came in to surrender. Among them was Red Eagle. He said to Jackson:

I am in your power. Do with me what you please. I am a soldier. I have done the white people all the harm I could. I have fought them, and fought them bravely. If I had an army, I would yet fight, and contend to the last. But I have none; my people are all gone. I can do no more than weep over the misfortunes of my nation.

Jackson admired Red Eagle's courage. He told him he could return home, but if he went to war again, and was captured, he would be executed. The Creeks, the General continued, would be safe only if they submitted unconditionally to Jackson's authority. Red Eagle replied he would do what he could to persuade any Creek holdouts to give up. He failed to accomplish that. The Seminole Indians, although once Creek in part, were now separate and independent. They said the Creeks had no right to speak for them. When the War of 1812 ended, Red Stick retired to a farm and lived in obscurity for the rest of his days.

As for Jackson, the Creek War raised him to a high peak on the nation's honor roll. It made this frontiersman's reputation as a military leader. To Westerners, he became the symbol of glory, one of "nature's noblemen," the ideal type for men to emulate. But although the war boosted his popularity, it ruined his health. The

*Chief Red Eagle, leader of the Creek Indians,
surrendering to General Jackson. The engraving
was made years later in 1859.*

eight months on the march in the wilderness, the battles,
the poor rations, the lack of medicine, were all devastating. Jackson suffered chronic diarrhea and dysentery,
and the pain caused by the wounds of the Benton gun-
fight brought him close to collapse many times. Yet he
never thought of sparing himself, always grimly pushing
himself even harder than he pushed his young soldiers.

In June the government gave Jackson his reward: the
rank of major general in the U.S. Army, and made him

commander of the Seventh Military District, embracing Tennessee, Louisiana, the Mississippi Territory, and the Creek Nation. He was instructed to return to Fort Jackson and negotiate a peace treaty with the Creeks.

Negotiate? Jackson didn't negotiate; he gave orders. He summoned the Creek chiefs, both the friendly and the hostile, to him at the fort and laid out what he demanded of them. If they failed to come, he threatened destruction. Leaders of the warring Creeks expected tough treatment. The Creeks who had fought alongside Jackson's troops expected a reward for their loyalty. But Jackson paid little attention to the friendly Creeks. Instead, he accused the entire Creek Nation of the crime of war against the United States. The cost of that war must be paid for, he said, and paid in full. The price, he figured, came to 23 million acres of land, or half the ancient Creek domain. The territory amounted to three-fifths of the present state of Alabama and one-fifth of Georgia. Jackson drew no distinction between the lands of the friendly and the hostile; about half the land he demanded belonged to Creeks who had fought under his flag.

The Creeks, he said, must also cut all ties with the British and the Spanish and accept the right of the United States to build roads through Creek lands and to open military and trading posts wherever needed.

The Indians were stunned. They had dealt with the whites before and knew how harsh they could be. But these terms were far worse than anything they expected. After the interpreter completed the translation of Jackson's speech, the Creeks went into private session to discuss the treaty offered them. The next day they urged Sharp Knife—as they now called Jackson—to ease his brutally unjust terms. They pointed out that most of the chiefs present had been his allies. But Jackson was adamant. By tonight, he warned, you must decide. If you reject the treaty, you will prove yourselves to be enemies of the United States.

Again the chiefs took council. What choice did they have? They knew Sharp Knife's overwhelming power and their own weakness. On August 9, 1814, thirty-five chiefs (only one of them was a Red Stick) signed the vengeful treaty. Professor Remini sums up the effect of Jackson's policy:

> *What Jackson had done had the touch of genius. He had ended the war by signing a peace treaty with his Indian allies! Most of the surviving Red Sticks had fled to Florida and planned to continue their warfare. Thus Jackson had converted the Creek civil war into an enormous land grab. Moreover, he insured the ultimate destruction of the entire Creek Nation. All the other southern tribes would one day experience the same melancholy fate at the hands of General Andrew Jackson.*

Later, when Jackson bid at public auction for some of the lands in the Creek region taken by the U.S. government, no one would bid against him. He got them at the lowest possible price.

The land seized from the Creeks assured the prosperity of the white planters. A vast and valuable acreage had been added to the expanding cotton kingdom. Jackson's treaty with the Creeks also fractured the Indian tradition of communal landholding, for it provided for individual ownership of land. The result was to split Indian from Indian, bribing some with land, shutting others out. It introduced them to the intense competitiveness of the Western economic system. In Jackson's view that meant fitting the Indians to enter "civilization."

6

THE BATTLE OF
NEW ORLEANS

The defeat of the Creeks was a major victory for the United States in the War of 1812. But it didn't mean that the war with Great Britain was over. In the summer of 1814, after beating Napoleon on the continent, the British sent 14,000 troops across the Atlantic for a renewed offensive against the Americans. They planned a three-pronged attack—against Lake Champlain in the north, Chesapeake Bay in the middle, and New Orleans in the south.

In August a force of 4,000 British veterans marched unopposed on Washington. (The panic-stricken government of President Madison and the Army had fled to Virginia.) The British set fire to the Capitol, the president's mansion, and most of the public buildings, as well as several private homes.

Deep gloom settled on the Americans that autumn. Would the British take back the country they had lost less than a generation ago? General Jackson, however, was sure that he could more than match the enemy if given the chance. He could never forget the sufferings he and his family had endured from the British during the Revolutionary War. "I owe to Britain a debt of retaliatory vengeance," he wrote Rachel from Mobile, where he had established headquarters. "Should our forces meet I trust I shall pay the debt. She is in conjunction with Spain arming the hostile Indians to butcher our women and children."

But the U.S. was fighting Britain, not Spain, which had declared itself neutral in this war. True, the U.S. was disputing with Spain the boundaries of Florida, a territory Spain had owned for a long time. Madison hoped to strengthen peaceful ties with her. Yet Jackson took it on himself to intimidate Spain. He wrote to warn the Spanish governor of Pensacola to arrest the "refugee banditti" from the Creek Nation who had fled into Florida and to punish them for their "crimes." Then he headed south to see that his demands were satisfied.

Meanwhile British naval and land forces had launched an expedition to invade the U.S. from the Gulf of Mexico. They expected Indians and Spanish would join them to drive the Americans back from the coast, giving the British control of New Orleans and the Mississippi Valley. The effect would be to contain the United States by British power on the north, the west, and the south.

Like most Southwesterners, Jackson wanted to take over Florida. He saw the war as an opportunity to conquer that territory. He asked Washington for permission to attack Pensacola because it was being used by the British as a base of operations—but he got no reply. So without orders, on November 7, he stormed the town with 3,000 men. The Spaniards surrendered and the English departed. Now Jackson felt he was in a better position to defend New Orleans.

On December 1, 1814, he moved his forces into New Orleans, expecting the British would soon attack the city. No preparations had been made for defense; no supplies or even arms were on hand. On the day of his arrival, a local resident noted the General's appearance:

A tall, gaunt man, very erect, with a countenance furrowed by care and anxiety. His dress was simple and nearly threadbare. A small leather cap protected his head, and a short blue Spanish cloak his body, whilst his high dragoon boots were long innocent of polish or blacking. His complexion was sallow and unhealthy; his hair iron grey and his body thin and emaciated like that of one who had just recovered from a lingering sickness. But a fierce glare lighted his bright and hawk-like eye.

Jackson gave the next two weeks to surveying the terrain. New Orleans at that time sat about 100 miles above the mouth of the Mississippi. The land downriver was made up of cypress swamps alive with alligators, muskrats, and pelicans. Where the soil would not support trees, razor-edged marsh reeds sprang six feet into the air. Streams and lakes offered at least six possible approaches to the city, with the great river the main one. Jackson's military problem was how to best defend all six routes. He sent out work crews to cut down trees and build barriers to the smaller water entries, and he stationed gunboats on the lakes and the river to patrol for signs of enemy movements. He had the planters put their slaves to work building batteries for his guns.

On December 15 couriers brought bad news. British vessels had captured Jackson's gunboats on Lake Borgne, one of the approaches to the city. Rumors flew that the British forces numbered 10,000 men, while Jackson had only 1,000 regulars and about 2,000 militia. As panic seized the city, Jackson swiftly declared martial law. Too weak from dysentery to stand, he lay on his couch at headquarters on Royal Street and issued orders through his aides, turning the city into an armed camp. "I am prepared to die in the last ditch before the enemy shall reach the city!" he said.

His decisive actions reassured the citizenry and their fear subsided. In the streets people sang "Yankee Doodle" and the "Marseillaise." Jackson tried every means to strengthen the city's defense. In those early years of the republic, blacks were almost totally excluded from militia units. But in Louisiana free African Americans had given distinguished military service under both the Spanish and the French. Jackson badly needed soldiers, and he accepted the support of two battalions of "Free Men of Color," placing them under white officers. His decision upset whites who feared a bloody revolt by blacks with guns. Nonsense, Jackson replied, they'll make excellent soldiers.

Both the English and the Americans courted the pirates who for many years had launched their notorious raids out of Barataria Bay, south of New Orleans. When the English tried it first, Jackson denounced them for seeking an alliance with "pirates and hellish banditti." The pirate chief, Jean Lafitte, saw greater advantage in lining up with the Americans, upon which Jackson called his men "privateers and gentlemen" and welcomed them to his side.

That the Battle of New Orleans would come out as it did seemed almost a miracle. No one (but Jackson?) expected a brilliant victory at New Orleans. The General's luck was fabulous; everything turned almost magically in his favor.

It took the British a week to disembark their 8,000 veterans. Then, without being detected, an advance guard of 1,800 redcoats moved up to a plantation only seven miles below New Orleans, an area which Jackson had left unguarded. The British general, John Keane, was urged by his officers to push forward to the city, confident that a surprise attack would succeed in capturing New Orleans. But Keane, who would make many wrong decisions, was too timid and decided to wait for the main body to come up and reinforce him.

Surprised at the news of the British advance, Jackson swore he would smash them that very night. With 2,000 troops, he rushed toward the plantation and early the next morning attacked. The result was a draw, measured by casualties on both sides, but Jackson's aggressive move had managed to halt an invasion that could probably have taken the city.

The day after this engagement, Jackson moved his army back a mile on a broad, flat plain, and set up defenses behind a canal—really a ditch four feet deep and ten feet wide—that ran from the eastern bank of the Mississippi to a cypress swamp about three-fourths of a mile away. He built earthen ramparts above it and placed his artillery at regular intervals.

The British came up close with about 7,000 men, to face the Americans' 3,000. The commanding officer was now General Edward Pakenham, a veteran of the Napoleonic Wars. His cannon and artillery on New Year's Day of 1815 began a heavy bombardment of the American positions. In two hours of steady fire, the British were outgunned; they failed to breach the American line.

Pakenham then came up with an unworkable plan. He would hurl all his power straight ahead through the Americans' well-prepared fortifications. It meant committing thousands of his redcoats to a frontal assault in the hope that their superior numbers would shatter the American resistance.

At dawn on the eighth of January, the British made their grand but foolish assault. In close ranks, the files of soldiers made two direct attacks in the face of deadly rifle and artillery fire. All the Americans had to do was shoot them down as they came. Within minutes, the entire advance crumbled into confusion. Commands to reform ranks and attack again were ignored by redcoats whose nerve was broken. When Pakenham and two other senior officers were killed, the British broke completely and fled the field.

In the first stage of battle, General Jackson moved back and forth behind his line, making sure every necessary measure was taken and shouting encouragement to his men. Then as the armies became fully engaged, he stood on elevated ground behind the center of the line so he could survey the whole sweep of the action and issue orders where needed. It was Old Hickory once more: calm, determined, inspiring his men with confidence in victory.

The battle lasted two hours, with the heart of the attack taking only thirty minutes. The casualties were remarkably uneven. Jackson lost 13 dead, 39 wounded,

General Jackson encouraging his troops during the Battle of New Orleans in 1815.

★

and 19 missing in action. The British: 291 killed, 1,262 wounded, and 484 captured or missing. The British withdrew to the safety of their ships and soon sailed away.

It was the last major engagement of the War of 1812. On January 8, the day of the Battle of New Orleans, no one this side of the Atlantic knew that on Christmas Eve, 1814—two weeks before the battle—American and British ministers in Ghent, Belgium, had signed a treaty of peace ending the war.

The British had lost any desire to support the huge, costly force it would take to fight the long war required to conquer the United States, and their people were grumbling over rising taxes. The British were ready to make a deal. The peace simply provided for a return to the situation that had existed before the war. Both countries accepted the prewar territorial boundaries. Neither side gained or lost anything. Both agreed to settle issues later. What the peace accomplished was a reconciliation between Britain and its former colonies. But in effect, America had won its second War of Independence.

News of the victory at New Orleans reached Washington at about the same time as the news of the peace treaty. Although New Orleans was the greatest land victory of the war, it had had no effect upon the war's outcome. What the victory did do for the Americans was to restore national pride, which had been badly shaken by repeated military failures and by the capture and burning of Washington.

Internal squabbles over the war had come close to wrecking the constitutional government. New England merchants had openly traded with and loaned money to Britain. Some of that region's leaders, late in 1814, had met at Hartford, Connecticut, and threatened to leave the Union unless constitutional amendments gave them veto power over certain commercial questions and the admission of new western states to the Union. It was only the Ghent Treaty that ended the threat of possible secession.

The power of Britain would never again overawe America, nor would the two nations ever again war against one another. America had proved to itself that it would endure. No longer could it be viewed as an experiment that might fail. It had earned respect abroad too, and would be recognized as an equal in the family of nations.

And Jackson himself? From now on, it seemed he could do no wrong. Towns and counties were named after him, and songs were written about him. One of the most popular songs was "The Hunters of Kentucky," sung or whistled everywhere. Such lyrics as these, sung on the stage, always roused tremendous applause:

> *But Jackson he was wide awake, and*
> *wasn't scared with trifles,*
> *For well he knew what aim we take*
> *with our Kentucky rifles;*
> *So he marched us down to Cyprus Swamp;*
> *The ground was low and mucky;*
> *There stood John Bull, in martial pomp,*
> *But here was old Kentucky. . . .*

The myth that had been growing for years took even deeper root. Military glory made Jackson a popular hero. And as it would do for many victorious generals to come, it eventually put him in the White House.

7

"ANY GOOD INDIAN
IS A DEAD INDIAN"

★

With the British beaten, Jackson marched his troops back to New Orleans. The whole city turned out to cheer the man who had saved their lives, their fortunes, and their honor. Through the temporary arch erected on the public square in front of the cathedral walked the "Hero of the Battle of New Orleans" as artillery thundered a salute. At the cathedral, children placed a laurel crown on the head of the "sublime savior." Jackson responded with a brief speech thanking the brave soldiers who "so effectually seconded my exertions for the preservation of their country."

President Monroe congratulated the General, and Congress thanked him with the award of a gold medal. In mid-March, Rachel and their adopted son Andrew arrived in New Orleans. At a grand ball given in the General's honor, he drew his wife out on the floor, where they performed a country dance. It amused a witness: "To see these two figures, the General, a long, haggard man, with limbs like a skeleton, and Madame la Générale, a short, fat dumpling, bobbing opposite each other . . . to the wild melody of 'Possum up de Gum Tree,' and endeavoring to make a spring into the air, was very remarkable, and far more edifying a spectacle than any European ballet could possibly have furnished."

Soon after, the Jacksons left for home. They were "feasted, caressed, idolized" at every stop on the way.

Rider and horse in their finery: a popular lithograph of the "Hero of New Orleans." Both Jackson and his horse seem to be made of wood.

Nashville itself gave Jackson a wild reception. The General settled again into plantation life. The government restructured the Army into northern and southern divisions, giving Jackson command of his region, with General Edmund P. Gaines as his second-in-command, to handle the details. In every way, life was made comfortable for Jackson. He was allowed to use the Hermitage as his military headquarters, so that he could oversee Army affairs while at the same time running his plantation and racing his stable. His pay as major general plus his allowances added up to a good, steady income for an honored country gentleman. More, it enabled him to pay off debts that had hung on him for many years.

Public curiosity would not be satisfied with the little known about Jackson beyond his military achievements. To satisfy a flood of inquiries (and perhaps with an eye to his political future), Jackson commissioned a friend to go through his papers and write a biography. Interest was high not only in the South but in New England. For there even Federalists whose political influence had dimmed because of their role in the Hartford Convention were speculating on switching allegiance to this rising Republican. Already many were urging Jackson to become a candidate for president.

Jackson's main concern at this time was dealing with the Indians of the region under his command. (A fusion of several tribes or groups, they were now called the Seminole.) Government agents visited the Indians to work out land settlements in compliance with the many treaties the government had signed. The most troublesome in Jackson's view was Article IX of the recently confirmed Treaty of Ghent. It called for returning to the Indians all possessions taken from them after the year 1811. So the 23 million acres Jackson had forced the Creeks to give over at the end of the Creek War had to be given back.

Did Jackson respect the obligation? No. Never. He had demonstrated his iron will many times before this. Perhaps the experience of exercising absolute and arbitrary power under the martial law he imposed on New Orleans made even more rigid his determination to have things his own way. The exhilaration of military success and the flattery that follows rarely have a good effect upon generals. Jackson would casually ignore the treaty provision and go on with his policy of removing the Indians from the surrendered territories. And the U.S. government would do nothing to stop him.

Jackson's first military goal was to protect the Southern frontier by routing the Spanish out of Florida. As long as the Spanish held their province, the Indians were sure of a safe haven. When the War of 1812 ended, the British left a fort on the eastern side of the Apalachicola River in Florida. It was about sixty miles below the American border. The fort was heavily stocked with guns and ammunition, including several cannon. Free blacks, descended from runaway slaves and many intermixed with Indians, had been living in the region for generations. With the British gone, they made the fort their headquarters. Their farms and grazing lands stretched fifty miles up and down the river. Over 300 of them, including women and children, garrisoned the earthen fort, with perhaps another thousand living in the surrounding region.

The Negro Fort, as it was called, drew to the safety of its walls restless slaves from the plantations of Georgia and Alabama. The slaveholders along the border complained bitterly when they saw their valuable human property drained away. The Army men stationed along the Southern frontier—many of them, like Jackson, slaveholders too—listened sympathetically. They wanted authority to destroy the Negro Fort that sheltered black "outlaws," "pirates," and "murderers," as the whites termed them.

But what could be done when the Negro Fort was deep inside Spanish territory? Some excuse was needed to violate the Spanish border and wipe out the black stronghold.

In Jackson's view, no excuse was needed. In May 1816 he wrote General Gaines:

> *I have little doubt of the fact that this fort has been established by some villain for the purpose of rapine and plunder, and that it ought to be blown up, regardless of the ground on which it stands; and if your mind shall have formed the same conclusion, destroy it and return the stolen negroes and property to their rightful owners.*

How could Jackson so easily accuse the African Americans of committing awful crimes from a point sixty miles south of the United States? The truth was, they were glad to stay away from the white Americans. As for "stolen negroes," they had stolen only themselves in running away to freedom. No rule of international law permitted Jackson to order that a fort in foreign territory be blown up and its people, now free citizens of Spain, be turned into slaves.

What governed Jackson were but two facts: the slaveholders' desire to enslave or kill blacks enjoying their lives in freedom, and his knowledge that Spain was too weak to protect its citizens.

On General Gaines's order, in July 1816, Navy gunboats headed up the river toward the Negro Fort. The intention was to provoke fire from the fort that would provide the excuse for its destruction. From inside the fort came word that its defenders would fire on any ships that tried to pass them. If they could not hold the fort, they meant to blow it up.

The Americans called on them to surrender, and the blacks opened fire. The guns on the U.S. ships answered

back from the river. A shell whizzed over the earth-
works and slammed into the fort's central powder maga-
zine. Hundreds of barrels of gunpowder exploded,
blowing the fort into pieces. When the Americans landed,
they found 270 burned and mangled bodies—men,
women, and children—and took 64 prisoners, only a few
of them uninjured. These survivors were taken to Georgia and given to men who claimed to be the descendants of
planters who generations before had owned the ances-
tors of these prisoners. No proof of identity was asked
for. The prisoners were simply delivered upon claim.

The Spanish government protested the invasion and
asked for the return of the property captured. The
Americans answered that it had belonged to the blacks,
from whom it was taken in conquest, and not to the
Spanish crown.

The unlawful aggression not only went unpunished;
it was rewarded. Twenty-two years later Congress paid
a bonus to the officers and crews of the gunboats who
had committed massacre and piracy.

By now it was clear that Jackson had fixed ideas
about the place of Indians in American life. Their place
was to be anywhere the whites were not. And his policy
would prevail. If anyone disagreed with him—even a
president—he would ride roughshod over the protests.

Jackson told off William H. Crawford, the secretary
of war and a man with presidential ambitions, when in
1816 Crawford ruled in favor of Cherokees who said that
4 million acres of the land taken from the Creeks in the
Fort Jackson treaty belonged to *them*. White settlers on
these acres joined Jackson in threatening political retalia-
tion. Crawford backed off, appointing Jackson (the fox in
the henhouse) to head a commission of three to reopen
discussion with the Cherokees and others.

With an offer of $180,000, and some bribery on the
side, Jackson got the Cherokees to sign a treaty under
which they gave up a vast tract of land. The U.S. also

promised lasting peace and friendship with the Cherokee nation. Jackson did the same with the Chickasaws in a treaty that threw open to white settlers land that stretched from Tennessee to the Gulf of Mexico. Of course, settlers poured in at once, as Jackson and his Tennessee friends borrowed heavily from western banks to finance their own speculation in these lands.

Soon after, the General engineered another treaty with the Cherokees that laid the groundwork for the government's removal of the Indians to west of the Mississippi River, beyond the states and territories of the United States. Jackson insisted that his own interpretation of earlier treaties with the Cherokees—which conflicted sharply with theirs—be accepted. He made threats that if they were stubborn, he would do to them what he had done to the Creeks. It worked.

In July 1817, the Indians gave up 2 million acres in Georgia, Alabama, and Tennessee, in return receiving the same amount of land on the west side of the Mississippi. Each Cherokee who was removed west would get a rifle, ammunition, one blanket, and one brass kettle or beaver trap. To help them move, the U.S. would supply flat-bottomed boats and provisions.

Jackson was convinced that so long as there were Indians on the U.S. frontier, there would be trouble. He believed the Native Americans had to be removed. But how? To exterminate them ("Any good Indian is a dead Indian") would outrage world opinion. The only solution was to uproot them and ship them off somewhere—to the farthest parts of the continent. Then they wouldn't be in the way. Where was that "somewhere"? The Great Plains of the West. But those lands had for untold generations been the home of the Plains Indians. Would they be glad to see strange tribes move in on them?

We don't know if Jackson ever gave that a thought. Or if he did, whether he cared. When he would become president, he would have his policy made into law. Any

Native Americans who remained on their ancestral lands, honoring their heritage, would be declared criminals.

To jump ahead for a moment: Jackson took another step toward Indian removal in 1820, when he negotiated a treaty with the Choctaws. He met with them in the Mississippi Territory. You've got to go if you wish to remain Indians, he said. If you don't move, he warned, "you must cultivate the earth like your white brother. You must also, in time, become citizens of the United States and subject to its laws." That meant the Indians would have to subject themselves too to the laws of the states where they lived. They knew the ruthless policy of those states toward Indians—crushing their culture and trampling over their rights.

Pushmataha, a Choctaw chief. Jackson forced the Choctaw to surrender their claim to more than 5 million acres of land in what is now west central Mississippi. Dying soon after, Pushmataha was buried in the Congressional Cemetery in Washington, D.C.

When the Choctaws argued against Jackson, he threatened them. Accept my offer, he said, or your nation "will be destroyed." They gave in; how could they match his power? They handed over some of the best, the most fertile land in the country—the heart of the Mississippi Delta region. No wonder the state of Mississippi would name its capital Jackson.

What about Florida? The question of taking it over somehow, that was still to be settled. It looked easier now that Spain's colonies down the whole length of Latin America were beginning to revolt. The administration hoped to add to that pressure by twisting Spain's tail in Florida. Jackson was just the man to do it. He knew he had backing in the highest places. Hadn't Secretary of State James Monroe written him after Pensacola: "I was not very severe on you for giving the blow, nor ought I have been for a thousand considerations, which I need not mention." Only months later, as whites swarmed into the area, Monroe—now president-elect—wrote how pleased he was: "As soon as our population gains a decided preponderance in those regions Florida will hardly be considered by Spain as part of her dominions." Monroe was assuming Spain would be ready to make a deal for the sale of Florida.

Jackson soon found the excuse for moving again on Florida. Runaway slaves had continued to filter into Spanish territory after the Negro Fort was destroyed. They joined blacks scattered across the peninsula almost to St. Augustine. Many found shelter in villages built up by the Seminole people.

General Gaines had placed his headquarters at Fort Scott, just north of the Florida border and near the Seminole village of Fowltown. Its chief warned Gaines to keep his soldiers away. Ignoring this challenge, Gaines sent an expedition into Fowltown on November 12, 1817. His soldiers drove the Indians into the swamps, killed and wounded many, looted the village, and then burned it down. Nine days later, the Indians took revenge. They ambushed a large open boat coming up the Apalachicola River, with forty soldiers, seven women, and four children aboard. They killed all but four men, who escaped by jumping overboard and swimming off, and one woman, whom they took captive.

The press blazoned the news of the massacre. Editors denounced it as an "unprovoked" attack. No mention was made of the massacre at the Negro Fort or of the killings at Fowltown. The result was to whip the white public into a rage against the Seminole.

Jackson hurried to get the bloody mess over with by seizing Florida. Late in December 1817, President Monroe let him know he could go ahead: "This day's mail," Monroe wrote, "will convey to you an order to repair to the command of the troops now acting against the Seminoles, a tribe which has long violated our rights, and insulted our national character. The movement will bring you on a theatre when possibly you may have other services to perform. . . ."

In March 1818, after a long march, Jackson arrived at Fort Scott and began his campaign against the Indians with a force of 3,500 men. About 2,000 were Creek warriors; the rest, regulars and militia. With his greatly superior numbers, Jackson was able to destroy several Seminole towns. Then he headed for St. Mark's, a Spanish fort Indians and blacks were using as an arsenal and headquarters, with or without the Spanish commander's permission.

Capturing the fort, Jackson picked up in it a Scottish trader, Alexander Arbuthnot, seventy years old, long known for his friendly relations with the Florida Indians. At the Suwanee River, Jackson captured Robert Armbrister, thirty-three, a veteran of the British Marines, who had helped train black warriors. Jackson ordered a court-martial for these two men, whom he labeled "foreign agents." With no evidence produced against either man, they were both declared guilty of stirring up the Creeks to war against the United States and sentenced to death. The court reconsidered Armbrister's case and reduced his sentence to fifty lashes and a year at hard labor. Jackson did not like this change of heart and ordered both prisoners executed. Two Indian leaders were lured aboard an American ship by the display of a British flag. They were made prisoners, and hanged on Jackson's orders. It was done without regard for American law, and by a very questionable trick.

Two chained Seminole Indian leaders are led to the gallows, where they would be hanged on Jackson's orders.

On May 28, Jackson's troops took Pensacola. (He got word to Monroe that if Monroe would only let him take some troops and guns, Jackson would take Cuba "in a few days.") After only a few months, Spanish Florida was in American hands. The General was more than ever the idol of the Army and the white settlers of the South.

But it had happened so fast that it was hard for the Monroe administration to digest. The president's Cabinet and Congress argued over whether to censure Jackson for violating the Constitution and assuming the power to make war. The debate in Congress was the first lengthy congressional investigation in American history. Some condemned Jackson, but most praised him. Only a few had anything to say about the reason the war was begun. Among them was Congressman Charles Storrs of Connecticut. Speaking to the House he said:

> *We profess to be the only free government on earth—that our intercourse with foreign nations is characterized by moderation and justice—that our institutions are pure and unspotted—that our national character is beyond reproach. Above all, we profess to be Christians. Go—follow the track of this Christian army through the Floridas. It can easily be traced. Every footstep is trodden in blood. The path is strewed with the unbleached bones and livid carcasses of its slaughtered inhabitants. Survey this frightful waste of human life—the awful calamities which have been inflicted on our own species, and say if our posterity will not blush for their ancestors. . . .*

The chief concern in Washington was that Jackson's swift invasion would upset the delicate maneuvers of the diplomats negotiating with Spain to acquire Florida. But hardly a year after Jackson's invasion, Monroe's secretary of state, John Quincy Adams, had little trouble getting Spain to do what he wished. As the dickering proceeded, Adams was bothered by the fact that Florida would add another big chunk of territory to the slaveholders' domain. Nevertheless, he did as much as anyone but Jackson to acquire Florida.

Harassed by their own colonial troubles in Latin America, dreading more clashes with the backwoods "Napoleon," Jackson, and hoping to forestall an invasion of Cuba, the Spanish gave in. On February 22, 1819, the treaty was signed, ceding Florida to the United States for the sum of $5 million.

For the white land grabbers and slaveholders, it was a day of jubilation. For the Seminole and the blacks, it was a day of mourning.

8

"PRESIDENT? JUST ASK ME!"

Those five months in Florida and the eighteen months in 1813–15 were all the active military service Jackson ever saw. Brief as the Florida campaign was, it worsened Jackson's already poor health. He wrote Monroe: "I am at present worn down with fatigue and by a bad cough with a pain in my left side which produced a spitting of blood, have reduced me to a skeleton . . . so I must tender my resignation."

He returned to the Hermitage, to a large new home built of brick and oak to replace the old log blockhouse. On one side was a small brick building he used as an office, and on the other, the kitchen and the quarters of the household slaves. He hired an English gardener to lay out a broad lawn and flower beds.

The Jacksons' guest bedrooms were rarely vacant, and at table there were usually several visitors— politicians, army officers, judges, speculators, and strangers too, who came to the door with letters of introduction. The couple's two older wards were now cadets at West Point. But because they missed children at play around them, the Jacksons had adopted another boy, Andrew Jackson Hutchings, the six-year-old orphan of an old friend.

Another addition to the family circle was Ralph Earl, an itinerant portrait painter, who came from a family of eccentric artists. A good part of his living was made from

The "Tennessee Gentleman," one of Ralph Earl's many
paintings of Jackson, made around 1830. The president's
plantation home is seen in the background.

doing portraits of the General. Earl had married one of Rachel's nieces, but the bride died a few months later. Sorry for the wanderer who had never known a real home, the Jacksons took him into the Hermitage, where he would live for the next seventeen years.

Jackson's enjoyment of peace in his renewed home life was badly disrupted when a financial crisis broke in 1819. It was the first of a long series of nineteenth-century crashes which would do great damage to all sections of the economy. The panic soon became a major depression that would last for years. Many state banks failed, creating hardships for debtors. The three regions—South, West, and North—blamed one another for trying to take unfair advantage of their needs. The economic issues would have great influence on the politics of all three sections. The West believed the North was determined to withhold the capital needed to develop the frontier. The South believed the North and the West had joined forces to raid the federal treasury for money to finance grand plans for roads and canals and to force a protective tariff upon the country that would raise the price of nearly everything Southerners bought. The North feared a combination of West and South might block a protective tariff and drain away its factory workers with promises of cheap land in the West.

People with political ambitions would try to juggle these sectional issues so as to produce a combination that would gain supporters in all three sections, or at least avoid antagonizing too many voters.

The business crisis came at a bad time for Jackson. Building the new Hermitage had drained his cash. He had also loaned money to many people now unable to repay him. Desperate, he sued those who defaulted, hoping to regain at least some of his money. With old friends he had promoted the founding of the new city of Memphis on the bluff overlooking the Mississippi. They had spent a great deal on clearing the site, putting up buildings, laying out streets and squares. Before business could revive to bring him profits, Jackson had to get rid of his share of the investment. He had also plunged deeply into land speculation in Alabama, borrowing for it, and now it appeared he might lose thousands of dollars.

With so many personal troubles—financial and medical—Jackson repeatedly wrote President Monroe to let him give up his military command. Monroe finally answered, offering him the job of organizing the administration of Florida.

Expansion into that territory had already raised in Northern minds the specter of a stronger slavocracy. The issue stirred up the country when Missouri applied for admission to the Union as a slave state. A heated argument broke out over the matter of power. Up to now, an attempt had been made to keep an even balance between free and slave states. The balance at the moment was eleven slave and eleven free states. But if Missouri came in slave, the slave region would have a two-vote majority in the Senate. After a year of harsh debate, the Congress in 1820 reached the "Missouri Compromise." It was really more a stalemate than a compromise. Each side added one new state—Missouri coming in slave, and Maine, free. The law also drew a line through the rest of the Louisiana Purchase territory, barring slavery "forever" from north of the parallel of 36°30′—the southern boundary of Missouri.

To both sides, the outcome was only a truce. The struggle over slavery would go on until one side or the other would prevail. Jackson saw the Compromise from the point of view of a slaveholder. In a letter he wrote:

The Missouri question . . . will be the entering wedge to separate the Union. It is even more wicked, it will excite . . . to insurrection and massacre. It is a question of political ascendancy and power, and the Eastern interests are determined to succeed regard-

less of the consequences, the Constitution or our national happiness. . . . I hope I may not live to see the evils that must grow out of the wicked design of demagogues, who talk about humanity, but whose sole object is self-aggrandisement. . . .

Urged by his friends, Jackson agreed to take on the job of governor of the Florida territory. They reasoned he would have many patronage plums to hand out, and it would be a fine chance to acquire land cheaply. Jackson saw the new post as a way to counter criticism for his conduct of the Seminole War. He resigned from the Army in June 1821. It was the end of a much publicized military career, and the start of a new course that would carry him to even greater heights.

The Government House of Pensacola proved to be anything but a comfortable assignment. There were all kinds of troubles with the Spanish over the transfer of the territory to the United States. Jackson found that the most important officials of the territory had been already chosen by Washington, with no regard for his own preferences. But he pushed ahead by issuing decrees to solve administrative problems and to begin necessary reforms. Rachel, who had come with him to Pensacola, had him close down shops, bazaars, and gambling houses, and forbid fiddling and dancing on the Lord's day.

One of the more troublesome problems to reach Jackson's desk was a sensational dispute over a large inheritance. Jackson settled it in his own high-handed manner. "Sure of his motive," as one historian put it, "he had disregarded diplomatic obligations, evidence, law, propriety, and forms of procedure." Such things only enraged him when they hindered his impulse to act quickly and to exert to the full his power. The effect of his action was to help out the illegitimate children of a rich man who claimed they had been deprived of their inheritance rights.

Jackson's conduct of the drawn-out affair put him on the nation's front pages. It drove some congressmen to consider hauling him in for an investigation. But they soon thought better of clashing with a man of such enormous popularity. Reporting his side of the matter to Secretary of State Adams, Jackson wrote:

> *I did believe, and ever will believe, that just laws can make no distinction of privilege between the rich and poor, and that when men of high standing attempt to trample upon the rights of the weak, they are the fittest objects for example and punishment. In general, the great can protect themselves, but the poor and humble require the arm and shield of the law.*

A noble sentiment, but one which Jackson forgot when he dealt with Indians, or with blacks.

Jackson found the governorship small potatoes for a man of his caliber. It was irritating to handle petty squabbles every day. He was exhausted and close to collapse because of old injuries. One of the bullets lodged in his body often formed abscesses that led to massive hemorrhages. He had both chronic dysentery and malaria and was taking mercury and lead treatments which poisoned his system.

Jackson stayed with his job for scarcely three months. Pleading Rachel's poor health (not his own), he resigned the office. Pensacola sent off the Jacksons with an elaborate farewell dinner, and they arrived in Nashville to a handsome welcome home.

Jackson welcomed the prospect of living out his life at the peaceful Hermitage. It was expensively furnished with hand-painted wallpaper, French beds, the best table silver and costly cut glass. Jackson's sideboard was

★

loaded with fine wines and whiskey; guests would not go thirsty. In Florida, Rachel had taken a fancy to Spanish cigars, which doctors advised her would improve her health. When she lit up a cigar, it startled Eastern guests who weren't used to women smoking.

Rachel was fatter than ever, and now her breath came in wheezy gasps. But she was almost saintly in her diligent devotion to her adopted children and the many nieces and nephews who enjoyed the hospitality of the Hermitage.

Jackson, fifty-five but looking sixty-five, spent the first several months at home too sick to think of anything but the prospect of an early death. Meanwhile, Rachel took on some of his duties at the Hermitage plantation. When he was able once more to enjoy the long bouts of eating and drinking with their guests, they observed his deep affection for Rachel and the way she would calm him when he erupted in anger at some real or fancied grievance.

For Jackson, to feel better meant to do more. He rode from Nashville to Alabama to inspect his plantation at Melton's Bluff, near Florence. He had bought the large mansion and the land from John Melton, a pirate who had grown rich by robbing the boats passing along the Tennessee River. Included in the purchase price were sixty slaves (Jackson already had about a hundred at the Hermitage) who had been ruled by the horsewhip. Their rebellious mood was evident in an advertisement placed in a Nashville paper:

50 DOLLARS REWARD
RANAWAY from the plantation of Gen. Andrew Jackson in Franklin County (Ala.) . . . Gilbert, a Negro man, about 35 or 40 years of age, very black and fleshy, with a full round face, has a scar on one of his cheeks, but not recollected which.

When Jackson had learned of Gilbert's flight a few weeks earlier, he wrote his Alabama overseer this advice: "You know my disposition, and as far as lenity can be extended to these unfortunate creatures, I wish you to do so; subordination must be obtained first, and then good treatment."

But by the time Jackson reached Melton's Bluff, three more slaves were missing. He took charge, and soon all the runaways were recaptured. "Although I hate chains," he said, "I was compelled to place two of them in irons."

Returned home again, Jackson had time to think not only about his plantation but about national affairs. The twenty newspapers from all over the country that he subscribed to littered the floor of his study. Reading their lurid stories of political and financial scandals tormented him. He took to jotting down his thoughts about what troubled him—the gross misuse or outright theft of public funds, the bribery of officials in return for favors, the indifferent way people in office handled their responsibilities. Was the entire nation immoral? Was everyone corrupt? How could people place their private interests above the public good?

What upset him mightily—and many others too— were people who hungered so badly for political power that they abused their public office to acquire still more power. One of the worst examples was the common practice of a handful of congressional leaders ganging up in caucus to nominate the next presidential candidate. This was true of his own party, the Republicans, the party of Jefferson. Any man they chose for the highest office was certain to be elected president, because the rival party, the Federalists, had grown so weak it had no chance of winning the national election. Of course both parties had followed this practice for decades. But in the past it meant a real contest between the two parties.

Now, with one party so dominant, it made a joke of free elections. If these few congressmen, and not the American people, could make a president, the Constitution meant very little.

Was Jackson thinking of running for president himself? When he read in a New York paper that some of his friends wished he would, he said angrily, "Do they think I am such a damned fool? No sir; I know what I am fit for. I can command a body of men in a rough way; but I am not fit to be President."

Still at issue in party politics was a conflict of views that went back to the Founding Fathers. The basic question was whose interests would the national government serve? Alexander Hamilton the financial wizard had spoken for the well-to-do conservatives called the Federalists. They wanted to centralize authority, so as to place greater power in the national government and give the executive branch freer rein in administration.

On the opposing side had stood Thomas Jefferson, leader of the Republicans. That party feared too strong a federal government, defended states' rights, and wanted to keep down federal expenditures. Its followers were suspicious of the business class and were against granting it monopoly or special favors. If power became too concentrated at the center, they said, then corruption would be sure to set in.

Jackson's political views lined up with the Republicans. He was alarmed by what he saw and read about. Power was on the rise in Washington, big money was being spent on internal improvements, such as roads and canals, the hated Bank of the United States had been rechartered, the Northeast was demanding even greater tariff protection, and the tide of corruption was sweeping into every corner of the land. Now, with the national election of 1824 coming on, would another congressional caucus usurp the people's right to choose a candidate?

As Jackson's worries mounted, letters arrived urging him to permit his name to be advanced for the office of president. I won't say no, he replied, but neither will I seek the office. It will have to come to me. "I have never been a candidate for any office," he said. "I never will. But the people have a right to choose whom they will to perform their constitutional duties, and when the people call, the citizen is bound to render the service required."

In plainer words—just ask me.

Jackson's own state, of course, was first to boost its favorite son for the presidency. The state legislature, with Jackson's tacit permission, unanimously placed his name in nomination. At the same time, to bolster his candidacy, the legislators elected him to the U.S. Senate in the fall of 1823. So, "against my wishes and feelings," he said, he headed once more for Washington.

As soon as word got out that Tennessee had nominated Jackson for the presidency, support for his candidacy poured in from all over the country. His popularity was no secret, but his political cronies had not expected such wild enthusiasm. Especially with four other prestigious men already in the field: John Quincy Adams, Henry Clay, John C. Calhoun, and William H. Crawford.

Not everyone was enthusiastic; the other candidates had strong supporters too. About Jackson, the *New York Evening Post* commented sarcastically that if the U.S. were under martial law, General Jackson by all means would be the best man for president.

As the campaign for the White House geared up, Jackson took his seat in the Senate. He lodged at a modest boardinghouse and found himself much in demand at dinner and dancing parties. "There is nothing done here but visiting," he complained in one of his frequent letters to Rachel. "You know how much I was disgusted with those scenes when you and I were here [in 1815]." The truth was, Jackson enjoyed the atten-

tion, and instead of showing up in society with a toma-
hawk in one hand and a scalping knife in the other, as his
enemies had hoped, he spruced up in a pair of fine black
cashmere pantaloons and a dress coat with silk-lined
buttons.

Jackson could be found at his seat in the Senate as
often as any other man. He spoke much less than most,
however, taking the floor only four times in six months
for a total of some twenty minutes. Each time it was to
back bills supporting the military. He voted on all key
matters and helped pass bills for both internal improvements and a protective tariff. Both votes roused angry
protests from the South and would be used against him
politically.

During the sessions of the Senate, Jackson did his
best to control his hot temper. His rivals hoped he would
commit some violent act that would discredit him, but he
played the calm statesman, not the wild frontiersman.
Even when he was baited, he did not rise to it. His chief
assignment was to chair the Committee on Military Affairs. Senator Thomas Hart Benton—whose brother
had almost killed Jackson—served on the same committee. When they first came face-to-face again, Benton
bowed and Jackson held out his hand. It was an effective
public response to the charge that Old Hickory cherished
his hatreds and never forgave.

9

AN AGE OF OPPORTUNISM
★

By the time Jackson returned home from his first session in the Senate, all Washington knew there was a good chance he would become president. The election of 1824 was a wide-open contest among Republicans; the Federalist Party was dead. But neither was the Republican Party in good shape. Sectional conflicts were splitting it into rival factions.

Besides Jackson, there were four other candidates. John Quincy Adams of Massachusetts, the secretary of state, had the greatest experience in public service. Henry Clay of Kentucky, the majority leader of the House, like Adams, backed strong federal programs of economic development. John C. Calhoun of South Carolina was the secretary of war and the loudest spokesman for states' rights. William Crawford of Georgia, the secretary of the treasury, was the choice of the Republican caucus in Congress, but that old way of nominating a president had collapsed. Early in 1824, when some Republican congressmen called a caucus to select the party's nominee for president, only a fourth of the members showed up. All but the Crawford men had stayed away. They gave Crawford sixty-four votes, leaving but two for Adams and one for Jackson. The result made a joke of this method. Since there was nothing yet like a national party convention, the other candidates, including Jackson, were nominated by state legislatures or

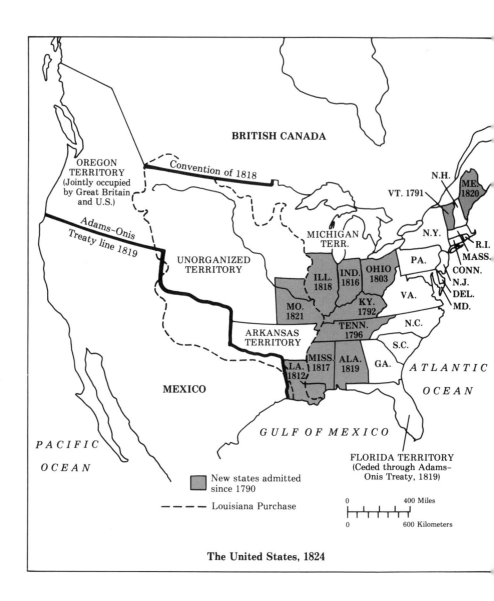

BRITISH CANADA

OREGON
TERRITORY
(Jointly occupied
by Great Britain
and U.S.)

Convention of 1818

Adams-Onis
Treaty line 1819

N.H.

VT. 1791

ME.
1820

UNORGANIZED
TERRITORY

MICHIGAN
TERR.

N.Y.

R.I.

MASS.

PA.

CONN.

ILL.
1818

IND.
1816

OHIO
1803

N.J.

DEL.

VA.

MD.

MO.
1821

KY.
1792

ARKANSAS
TERRITORY

TENN.
1796

N.C.

S.C.

MISS.
1817

ALA.
1819

GA.

ATLANTIC

MEXICO

LA.
1812

OCEAN

GULF OF MEXICO

PACIFIC

OCEAN

FLORIDA TERRITORY
(Ceded through Adams-
Onis Treaty, 1819)

New states admitted
since 1790

- - - Louisiana Purchase

0   400 Miles

0   600 Kilometers

The United States, 1824

mass meetings. When Jackson swept all before him in an early vote in Pennsylvania, Calhoun realized he had overestimated his strength and withdrew. He decided to join Jackson's forces as the vice-presidential candidate.

The engine powering Jackson's candidacy was a little group of Tennesseans. The lawyer John Overton was one of the West's wealthiest men; and Jackson's oldest friend, Senator John Eaton, had served under the General in the War of 1812 and had helped maneuver Jackson's appointment as governor of Florida. William B. Lewis was a close friend living on the plantation next to the Hermitage. A master politician, he knew how to start a movement in such a way as to make it look spontaneous and to win for it the prestige or popularity needed to produce the effect desired, at the right time and place. The candidate, meanwhile, would prepare to be caught up by the movement which, from the start, his manager plotted.

Lewis worked like the director of a play. He made political action into theater. Many important things were done behind the scenes, concealed from the audience. If necessary, he would have his star performer adjust the way he played the role, with a constant eye on the desired effect. The climax of the performance would be reached when the actor came down to the footlights and bowed to the "will of the people."

William G. Sumner describes Lewis and his function:

He had the great knowledge required by the wire-puller—knowledge of men, good judgment of the influences which would be potent, if brought to bear on each man or group. He knew the class amongst whom Jackson's popularity was strongest. He knew their notions, prejudices, tastes, and instincts. He knew what motives to appeal to. He wrote very well. When he wanted to go straight to the point he could do so. When he wanted to produce effects or suggest

*adroitly, without coming to the point, he could do that
too. He also knew Jackson well. . . .*

Lewis seems to have honestly loved Jackson. He threw
all his energies into trying to elect him president, yet he
showed no sign of selfish interest. He knew that if Jackson was uninformed on some matter and had no strong
prejudice regarding it, he could be swayed by someone
who had won his confidence and knew how to put a
question before him. Lewis would show again and again
that he could do that very well. A problem, however,
was that once Jackson's mind was made up, he could be
rigid. And to go against his opinion could break up a
friendship. Lewis had the tact to avoid that.

The political issues stressed most often in the newspapers were the tariff, internal improvements, Indian
removal, slavery, and territorial expansion. But voters
had a hard time figuring out where the candidates stood,
especially Jackson. His record on most issues up to now
had been so inconsistent that his operators, catering to
the local voters, in one state could say he was "pro-this"
or "anti-that," and in another state they could say just
the opposite. The one conviction they held consistently
was to defend slavery from political attack.

Anyhow, as Adams put it, all the Jackson people had
to do was to cry, "8th of January and the Battle of New
Orleans!" Don't commit yourself on anything, said Jackson's advisers. They pictured him before the country as
energetic, patriotic, courageous, decisive. Old Hickory
was the "Nation's Hero," the "People's Friend." The
aim was to inspire such confidence in the man that people
would not bother to ask what his views were on any
subject.

It was an age of opportunism. Many political leaders
—then as well as now—do not dream of great achievements that would make America a better place to live in.
They enter politics because they believe it to be one of

the surer paths to fame, to power, to wealth. Of course, there were dreamers and idealists in Jackson's time— there always are—but they were not among the party leaders; they were in the reform movements.

Jackson never spoke of exactly what drew him to a political career. Certainly the urge to increase his fortune was a strong motive. He was always writing his beloved Rachel to assure her he wanted nothing more than never to separate from her. Yet he did just that again and again, to advance his political career.

The parties and their candidates were concerned with political issues only insofar as they could attract voters. The fact that they often talked out of both sides of the mouth shows it was winning office that counted above all else. So they tried to be many things to many voters. (The one thing the Jackson people could not do was to make him out to be against slavery or for Indian rights.)

A myth that persists is that Jackson and his party contributed to extending democracy by broadening the suffrage. That happened well before the 1824 race. Most states had already lifted most restrictions on the suffrage of white male citizens or taxpayers. Jackson did not initiate those reforms; he benefited by them. During his own presidency, some further extension of the suffrage took place.

At the time of the 1824 election, the first Tuesday in November had not yet been set apart to allow the whole nation to vote on the same day. When the returns trickled in from the twenty-four states that made up the country, Jackson had the greatest number of popular votes. He led also in the electoral college, with ninety-nine votes. Adams came next with eighty-four, Crawford with forty-one, and Clay with thirty-seven.

Because no candidate had the required majority of the electoral votes, the presidential election was thrown into the House of Representatives. The Twelfth Amendment to the Constitution requires the House to choose between the three highest candidates. In such cases, each state had one vote determined by its delegation. Clay, with the lowest vote, was eliminated. Crawford, whom illness had paralyzed, was not a serious contender. The real choice lay between Jackson and Adams.

It was Henry Clay who would decide the outcome. He controlled the vote of the three states that he carried. On February 8, 1825, on the first ballot, seven states voted for Jackson and four for Crawford, while Adams got the votes of thirteen states, and won the election. It would be President Adams, not President Jackson.

At first Jackson took his defeat calmly. A few days later, he angrily charged that he had been cheated out of the presidency by a "corrupt bargain" between Adams and Clay. It's likely that his advisers put this idea into his head because they knew how useful the charge would be politically. It soon became known that before the House voted, Adams and Clay had met privately to discuss the situation. No one knows what they said. But when Adams announced, five days after the election, that Clay would be his secretary of state, it was easy to claim there had been a "corrupt bargain," that Adams had paid Clay off for his support. Clay said he voted for Adams because he didn't think a military hero was fit to be president.

Both Adams and Clay distrusted and disliked Jackson. Adams felt he needed Clay's support to get the West behind Adams's program in Congress. And Clay, who wanted desperately to be president himself, believed the State Department post would put him in line for it. It didn't work out that way. Jackson's charge that Clay was a "Judas" for blocking his election stuck permanently to the Kentuckian. Clay had signed his own political death warrant. The voters would never put him in the White House.

*Henry Clay, painted by George P. A. Healy around 1845,
some twenty years after Clay cast the deciding vote in the
House that cost Jackson the presidency.*

Adams began his administration with an eloquent call
for national planning based upon a broad interpretation of
what the Constitution permitted. He asked support for
federal road and canal building, standardization of
weights and measures, the establishment of a national
university and a naval academy, promotion of commerce
and manufacturing, and governmental aid to science and
the arts.

John Quincy Adams, sixth president of the United States, was charged by Jackson with winning the office by a corrupt deal with Henry Clay.

★

Adams's program quickly fell victim to sectional conflicts and political infighting. Within a year, his administration was in deep trouble. Although a brilliant statesman, he was a poor politician. He failed to win more than a few supporters in Congress. A colorless man, he had no popular appeal and could not rally the country to pressure Congress. His four years in the White House were both unproductive and unhappy.

The Jackson people spearheaded the attack on Adams. If his government could exercise "such vast powers," as one senator asked, wouldn't it soon be meddling with slavery? That worry led them to oppose the president's request to take part with the newly independent republics of Latin America in a Panama Congress. The aim of Adams was to signal hemispheric solidarity and to block any effort by Spain to regain its lost colonies. But the Southerners in Congress feared the Latin Americans might oppose slavery and the slave trade. Even to sit down at the same conference table with Haiti would be indirect recognition of a nation created by a slave revolt. So many obstacles were put in the way that nothing came of Adams's proposal.

The Jackson people showed just as much loathing for the president's Indian policy. When Adams tried to protect the Creek and Cherokee Indians against ejection by Georgia, that state defied him, while Congress stood by. Settlers in Georgia, Mississippi, and Alabama were eager to get the millions of acres still belonging to the region's tribes, and they opposed whatever Adams tried to do on behalf of the Indians.

Jackson did not sit still and wait for the Adams-Clay faction to fall apart. He began scheming to capture the White House from Adams at the next election by making the biggest drive for the presidency that had thus far been attempted. A new political alliance began to take shape quickly. Calhoun joined up with Jackson to build opposition to the administration. When Jackson returned

---

home that fall, the Tennessee legislature promptly nominated him again for president. He resigned from the Senate to devote himself to his presidential campaign. His Nashville backers plotted a strategy for beating Adams in 1828. They formed a new party, soon to be called the Democratic Party. It was really the Jackson Party, and would remain so until his death, for its leaders listened to what he advised even after he had left the White House. In Congress the party was masterfully organized by Martin Van Buren, a New Yorker fifteen years younger than Jackson.

Descended from a long line of plain Dutch farmers in Columbia County, Van Buren, like Jackson, had learned the law as an apprentice. He used his practice as a springboard into public office. Jackson had launched his public career sponsored by the rich and powerful, but Van Buren had won success despite their opposition. He had held several state offices and built a powerful political machine in upstate New York. By the time he left Albany in 1821 to take a seat in the U.S. Senate, he was called "Sly Fox" or the "Little Magician," in recognition of his great skills as a political operator.

Van Buren brought into the Democratic Party the methods developed in New York politics. Everyone saw Jackson as the coming man; no one disputed his popularity. Van Buren knew how to make forceful use of that popularity. He and the Nashville men organized local Jackson committees up and down the country. Their job was to carry on propaganda for Jackson, to make known his services to the nation, to refute charges against him, to attack the Adams administration, and to swap information, ideas, and reports with one another and with a headquarters set up in Washington. They organized parades, rallies, and barbecues, and handed out hard liquor generously. They gave out buttons and hats with hickory leaves attached.

The headquarters was both a command center and

what today would be called a public relations agency. Staff writers drafted speeches, statements, and reports and fed material to editors of newspapers backing Jackson. Facts, slogans, arguments were hammered into the heads of the voters. So were slander and insult, aimed at the opponent. Partisan editors were not a new thing in politics, but now all over the country local papers, some small, some large, sprang up edited by men who pushed only one side of public questions. Bent on winning, they ignored facts, truth, fairness, justice.

This was the first time a formal campaign biography was created (*Life of Jackson*, by his friend, John Eaton) to promote a presidential candidate. A second innovation was the use of public opinion polls. Early in 1824, three pro-Jackson newspapers began polling voter preferences at public meetings. How honest were the methods used or the results reported we don't know. But such polling became a feature of elections. With them, the parties hoped to create a groundswell of public opinion in favor of their candidate.

Who were the voters the Democrats appealed to? Jackson said he spoke for "the humble members of society—the farmers, mechanics and laborers. . . ." The "common people," as they all liked to say, people with little money, people more likely to be debtors than creditors. It looked like this was a party of the poor because it was supported largely *by* the poor. But as the Jacksonian scholar, Edward Pessen, points out:

> *If this is taken to mean—as I think it often is—that a so-called party of the poor either truly serves them or that it deserves their support, then I think it is a false notion. It does not take into account the power of demagogy or the gullibility of the voters. To cite a drastic example, the fact that Hitler's party may have been supported by the German workers hardly makes the Nazis the party of the poor.*

What counts is not economic statistics or voting records but an evaluation of a party's *behavior*, Professor Pessen concludes. As for the "common man" himself running for president or even for Congress, there was small chance of that. The cost of running for Congress at this time was roughly $3,000—a sum that barred all but rich men, or men with rich friends. So while there were more rich men in the opposition party, most leaders of the Democratic Party were just as wealthy and successful. In the leadership of both parties, backgrounds, methods, and goals were commonly shared.

The aim of the Jackson people was to heat up the public temper for the next election. The nation had taken the results of 1824 calmly; it took some effort to create an uproar over the "corrupt bargain." The claim that Jackson had been cheated proved an effective way to do it, though no one could prove how he was cheated. It showed that if you hammered away with an accusation, you didn't need facts.

Adams himself took no steps to build support by awarding government jobs to friends. He appointed those he thought best qualified, regardless of party. He believed the Jacksonians were spending money to poison public opinion through the press, yet he would do no favors for editors on his side.

When a new Congress met in 1827, Adams's men were a minority in both the House and Senate. That was the first time in American history that a president found himself opposed in Congress by a majority from the other party. Most of that session was spent on making charges (chiefly about extravagance, and unfounded) against the Adams administration. There was no attempt by the Democrats to be fair or truthful.

10

THE PRESIDENT
AND HIS
KITCHEN CABINET

★

Presidential candidates in those times did not rush about the country making speeches, shaking hands, kissing babies. The day of creating endless "photo opportunities" was far in the future. The drumbeating for the party's choice was left to his henchmen. It was even unusual for a presidential hopeful to issue public statements, although Jackson did. His command of grammar was shaky, and most of his statements were written or revised by someone else. He would sit in the Hermitage and, as he said, leave his future "to the judgment of an enlightened, patriotic and uncorruptible electorate." This was stated in a private letter, carefully leaked to the press.

Early in the campaign, the Marquis de Lafayette arrived in Nashville. A hero of the American Revolution, in which he had served as aide to General Washington, the Frenchman was on a grand tour of the country he had helped win its independence fifty years ago. After hundreds of receptions and parades, to the cheers of millions, his large party stopped at the Hermitage to see Old Hickory. Lafayette's son-in-law noted "the simplicity of the house. I asked myself if this could really be the dwelling of the most popular man in the United States. We might have believed ourselves on the property of one of the richest and most skilled German farmers if, at every step, our eyes were not afflicted by the sad spec-

★

tacle of slavery." Lafayette made Jackson a gift of a pair of pistols given him by George Washington.

A few weeks later, Frances Wright, a Scottish-born heiress, young, beautiful, and devoted to social reform, dropped in on Jackson. She told him she wanted to establish a cooperative colony of black people that would be a halfway house between slavery and freedom. Her plan called for buying slaves who would form a commune and, with the help of a white staff, raise a cotton crop. Eventually, after paying back their purchase price, they would be set free and would move out of the country.

It was not an idea that would appeal to most African Americans. Why should they have to work off their purchase price when their labor had been forced from them in the first place? Jackson, like Jefferson and other slaveholders, feared free blacks and wanted them all to leave America. He sold Frances Wright a large tract of his land about thirteen miles up the Wolf River from Memphis. She bought a small number of slaves with her own money and started a commune she called Nashoba. When it soon failed, for many reasons, she took the slaves to Haiti, where they were welcomed to freedom with the gift of land and tools.

As the election campaign advanced, Jackson was faced with demands that he explain many questionable incidents in his past—such as the killing of Dickinson, the bloody tangle with the Bentons, the executions of Armbrister and Arbuthnot. But to Jackson, most painful and infuriating was the old charge about the circumstances of his marriage to Rachel. The story first appeared at length in a Cincinnati paper, was picked up by others all over the country, and was repeated in pamphlets. One of these asked, "Ought a convicted adulteress and her paramour husband to be placed in the highest offices of this free and Christian land?"

Jackson blamed Henry Clay for using gutter tactics and threatened his "destruction." It confirmed his belief

"*Jackson is to be President, and you will be HANGED.*"

*A campaign cartoon attacking General Jackson for his
casual way of hanging people. The message is: Vote for him
to be president and you, too, will be hanged!*

that Adams and Clay had stooped to a "corrupt bargain" to win power. Clay denied he had anything to do with it. Jackson's friends feared he would be goaded to some terribly rash act to avenge the insult to Rachel, "my aged and virtuous female."

Eaton begged Jackson to ignore the charge and just go on weighing and baling his cotton. But after asking Jackson to control his feelings and be silent, the Jackson editors had free rein to say what they liked. They called Adams a "stingy, undemocratic" aristocrat determined to destroy the people's liberties. They said he had been born out of wedlock and had lived with his wife before marriage. The Adams editors countered by calling Jackson the son of a prostitute, a brawler, a murderer, a drunkard, a gambler, and an illiterate.

The two parties swapped dirty blow for dirty blow right up to the election. (Such behavior occurs today, too.) The outcome was a victory for Jackson. It was the South that won the election for him. If he had not run up huge popular and electoral majorities in those states, he would not have been swept into office. Adams had an electoral and close to a popular majority of the votes of the states in the other regions.

The total vote did not go over the highest levels reached in elections before this one. There was no nationwide rush to the polls to put the self-proclaimed champion of democratic rights in the White House. In a nation of nearly 13 million, barely 1 million white males came out to vote. Jackson's victory was assured by Southern voters convinced he would defend the slaveholders' interests. All the campaign hullabaloo about private scandals didn't make them lose sight of the issue that mattered most to them.

When the news of Jackson's victory reached the Hermitage, Rachel said she was glad for his sake, but "for my part, I never wished it." Reluctantly, she went to Nashville to buy the clothes she would need as the

★

First Lady. She grew tired while shopping and stopped for a rest at a friendly editor's office. There, picking up a campaign pamphlet of the kind Jackson had kept from her, she was violently shocked to read the blunt language accusing her of adultery and bigamy. She sank to the floor and began to cry uncontrollably.

Her end was near. A bad cold came on, and soon after she suffered a heart attack. For the next four days, Jackson rarely left his wife's bedside as two doctors tried their best to save her. On the night of December 22, 1828, Rachel had another severe heart attack and died. Jackson sat by her bed for hours, hoping vainly for signs of returning life. He remained in her room all the next day, inconsolable, unable to speak. On Christmas Eve, with thousands of mourners attending, Rachel was buried in the garden of the Hermitage. "My heart is nearly broke," the president-elect said.

Rachel's death, supposedly of a heart broken by the slanders against her, made Jackson a kind of substitute martyr. The image of the "Iron Man" was tempered by stories of how he would sit in the White House with Rachel's portrait propped up before him, her open prayer book at his side, and weep.

On January 18, 1829, Jackson began the long journey to Washington by steamboat. With him went his nephew, Andrew Jackson Donelson, to serve as his secretary; Donelson's wife, Amy; Jackson's political adviser William Lewis; and a few others. Jackson was dressed in deep mourning—black suit, white shirt, black tie, black band on his arm and another on his tall beaver hat. At Cincinnati he got off the boat and walked through the crowd to his hotel. "He wore his gray hair carelessly but not ungracefully," said a bystander, "and in spite of his harsh, gaunt features, looked like a gentleman and a soldier."

That Jackson himself was a very sick man—many thought dying—was no secret. In addition to all his other injuries and ailments, he suffered splitting headaches now and his thin body was racked by a persistent cough. A lifelong tobacco habit probably did much to worsen his health. He smoked an old Indian bowl pipe with a very long stem, puffing out such great white clouds that visitors could hardly breathe. He chewed tobacco too, and would often spit during conversations or even while presiding over affairs of state.

Jackson's inauguration, on March 4, 1829, was one of the most memorable in American history. Some observers described it as the spontaneous outburst of popular pride in the first "people's president." Others viewed it as a sorry and disgraceful riot that wrecked the dignity traditional on this solemn occasion.

That Tuesday marked the end of a Washington winter so harsh that poor people were found frozen to death in the streets. The day dawned clear and mild, with about 20,000 people drawn to Washington to witness the great event. They packed in before the east portico of the Capitol, breaking into great cheers as Jackson appeared.

His Inaugural Address was brief, lasting only ten minutes. He spoke so low that only those in the first rows could hear some of his words. He straddled the issues of the tariff and internal improvements and promised to economize and wipe out the national debt. When he finished, he listened for a few minutes to the shouts of the crowd, then took the oath of office from Chief Justice John Marshall. Again the crowd screamed and yelled. Then Jackson rode down Pennsylvania Avenue to his new home, the White House. The huge crowd followed closely, eager to enjoy the promised public reception.

They overran the grounds and jammed into the White House itself. Everyone wanted to shake the president's hand and to get a share of the punch, the lemonade, the ice cream, and the cake. In no time, the

*The mob scene on the White House grounds as
Jackson was inaugurated in 1829. A caricature
engraved by Robert Cruikshank.*

festivities turned into a wild brawl. Waiters were
knocked down, tables overturned, the carpets filthied
with whiskey and tobacco juice. Women fainted, men's
noses were bloodied. Frightened by the danger to the
frail president's safety, a ring of his friends formed
around him and hustled him out a back door and into a
boardinghouse nearby. The mansion might have been
wrecked if tubs of punch had not been carried outside to
the lawn, the crowd following, some of them diving out
through the windows.

Well before the inauguration took place, Jackson had picked his cabinet. Cabinet members run their departments and advise the president. He need not take their advice; he need not even ask for it. The Cabinet discusses no more than the president wants it to discuss. Jackson's Cabinet was called one of the worst in that century.

He chose men from different parts of the country in the hope of uniting their various interests behind him. Van Buren of New York got the top post of secretary of state, and John Eaton, Jackson's old friend, the post of secretary of war. Others came from Pennsylvania, North Carolina, Georgia, and Kentucky.

Jackson treated them as executive officers and did not often hold Cabinet meetings. But he needed to lean on somebody. He chose such men from among friends, family, and even chose Van Buren, a Cabinet member. Most held no important public positions. Several were newspapermen. The old aristocracy that had ruled the country looked down on journalists as servants of their class, not as equals. Since journalists had helped Jackson win power, why not use them now?

This inner circle became known as the "Kitchen Cabinet." They included Amos Kendall, an editor, who worked on many of Jackson's state papers. Isaac Hill was another editor. Francis P. Blair ran the Washington *Globe*, whose chief function was to praise the administration, denounce its critics, and build the Democratic Party. And then there was William Lewis, who for years had labored to make Jackson president.

This shifting group plus others had considerable influence with Jackson. Their ideas helped shape administration policy. But they did not dictate what Jackson said or did. No, he was master in his own White House. He was the first to declare that "the President is the direct representative of the people" and speaks for them even more than Congress does. This belief would lead Jack-

Three of the key figures in Jackson's "Kitchen Cabinet": (right) Amos Kendall, postmaster general; (below left) Francis P. Blair, editor of the Washington Globe; and (below right) William B. Lewis, political manager.

son to appeal to the people over the heads of Congress. At such times, he would say he had brought the issue before the people "and I have confidence that they will do their duty." His notion of their duty was to support him in whatever he wanted to do. Yes, he knew the Constitution decreed that there be three equal parts of government—the legislative, the executive, and the judiciary—but he insisted that *he* was the first among equals.

His personal qualities account in part for the role he played in the White House. He dramatized himself as the hero opposing the elite. The Congress represented the elite (or the "special interests," as recent presidents have put it), while he, the president, was the voice of the people. His private correspondence reveals that he thought of himself as an emperor, accusing those who differed with him of betraying him the way Brutus had betrayed Caesar.

Jackson was not the kind of president, however, who limited himself to playing the role out front, onstage. He didn't nap during meetings or demand only one-paragraph summaries of complex issues. He was a strong-willed activist who wanted to get things done, even if always in his own way. He took firm control of the men who staffed the machinery of government, gave long hours to planning policy, and paid close attention to the details of execution. His salary was $25,000 a year, payable monthly.

With Rachel gone, the management of the White House and its eighteen domestic slaves fell to Emily Donelson, Andrew's wife. Married at seventeen, and only twenty now, she was good-looking, unaffected, and graceful. She was used to handling the responsibility of a large plantation home. The Donelsons and their three-year-old son were now the heart of Jackson's family. The White House became the home too for the painter Ralph Earl, to whom the president assigned a private studio.

And William Lewis, upon whom the president depended for so many services, agreed to move in from Tennessee. For his own living quarters, Jackson chose two rooms at the northwest end of the second story.

Jackson got out of Congress the funds to finish the incompleted White House and its interior decoration. The north portico was built, and single-story wings were extended to east and west from the center. These spaces were used as offices and stables. Later, Jackson had running water installed, and a formal garden laid out, where several magnolia trees were planted in Rachel's memory.

Jackson broke the social rules for presidential levees, or public receptions. Never before was there such a mix of all kinds of people. One guest, Harriet Martineau the English author, observed that "these singular and miscellaneous assemblages, threw together public officials, diplomats, and prominent local citizens whose clothes and hands were clean, with soldiers redolent of gin and tobacco" and "men begrimed with all the sweat and filth accumulated in their day's—perhaps their week's—labor." It gave the crowded drawing rooms, she said, "odors more pungent than agreeable." Judged by the standards of upper-class London, she thought most Americans were dirty.

Jackson ate sparingly and drank very little now. He gave up whiskey for himself though he bought it by the barrel for his guests. One of them was the brilliant Shakespearean actress Fanny Kemble, here from London on a tour. She described the president as she saw him in the White House:

> *Very tall and thin, but erect and dignified in his carriage . . . a good specimen of a fine old well-battered soldier. . . . His manners are perfectly simple and quiet, therefore very good; so are those of his niece, Mrs. Donelson, who is a very pretty person.*

11

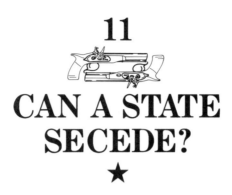

CAN A STATE SECEDE?

★

Long before he became president, Andrew Jackson spoke firmly against giving jobs to men solely because they belonged to the right party. That was in 1798. Again, in 1816, he urged President Monroe to ignore partisan politics in picking his Cabinet. "Choose characters more conspicuous for their capacity without regard to party," he said. He repeated that belief in 1825, when President Adams began his term.

Yet, when Jackson became president, he reversed himself. He gave men appointments to office just because they were loyal Democrats. He justified his switch by calling it an extension of democracy. Rotation in office would make the people feel they had a share in their own government. In his first annual message, he said that "The duties of all public officers . . . are so plain and simple that men of intelligence may readily qualify themselves for their performance." And he added that "No one man has any more intrinsic right to office than another." He was telling the voters that any one of them could fill those jobs. However, losing or getting a job depended on loyalty or lack of loyalty to him. He once said that "It is as true in politics as in morals that those who are not for us are against us."

Nothing made his enemies madder than this policy on appointments. The "spoils system," they labeled it. Jackson of course didn't call it "spoils." He called it reform. But one leading Democrat, William Marcy, said bluntly that winning politicians "claim as a matter of right, the advantages of success. They see nothing wrong in the rule, that to the victor belongs the spoils of the enemy." Jackson of course knew that anyone he appointed would feel more closely bound to the party that offered such a material reward. Patronage is what cements a party organization together.

The spoils system didn't begin with Jackson. The difference now? There were many more jobs to give away. Still, Jackson did not follow Marcy's rule as much as was charged. In his eight years in office, he would remove less than one-fifth of all federal officeholders. And some of these people were justly removed for incompetence or dishonesty. A gross example was Samuel Swartwout, appointed by Jackson to head the New York Customs Office. He stole over a million dollars from the public treasury. Although the rival party, the Whigs, attacked Jackson for the spoils system, once in office they did the same thing. Plainly, the spoils policy suited the mood and the needs of both major parties.

What was the long-term effect? In the words of Professor Glyndon Van Deusen, an historian of the Jackson era:

> *The spoils system was to prove a creeping blight through the years. It threatened paralysis of the national party organization because it inevitably increased the power of local political machines. It fostered the appointment of party hacks and the consequent degradation of the administration of government. The hero from the Hermitage must bear a heavy load of responsibility for the development of these evils in national government, although it is doubtful he perceived them. He saw administration in terms of individual officeholders, rather than as a process of government.*

The name Andrew Jackson became so identified with the spoils system that for many years his administration became its symbol. This political cartoon by Thomas Nast was part of Nast's unrelenting attacks upon the plundering of New York by Tammany Hall. Note that Jackson is riding not a horse but a hog.

With Jackson in such poor health as he took office, few thought he would be able to serve more than one term. Who would succeed him? One potential candidate was Vice President Calhoun. The other was Secretary of State Van Buren. Their rivalry made harmony within the administration difficult to maintain.

What made the rivalry worse was the "Eaton Affair." Jackson's close friend Secretary of War John Eaton was a rich middle-aged widower. He had taken up with the attractive, young Peggy O'Neal Timberlake, daughter of a local innkeeper, whose husband committed suicide soon after. Jackson advised Eaton to go ahead and marry her, even though she had a bad reputation in Washington. Marrying her, said Jackson, will disprove those charges and restore Peggy's good name.

The couple married in 1829, but the gossip didn't stop; it grew worse. Would Mrs. Eaton be received by Washington society? No, ruled Floride Calhoun. She would have nothing to do with Peggy Eaton, and the wives of many Cabinet members as well as most of Washington's elite followed her example. They would not attend White House receptions if Peggy Eaton was present. When Emily Donelson too refused to receive Peggy, Jackson asked her to leave the White House.

The president was furious with the women who ostracized Peggy, whom he liked. It must have reminded him of what scandal had done to his own Rachel. He even called a cabinet meeting to discuss Peggy's virtue, and pronounced her "chaste as a virgin." The Cabinet was stunned to have such an affair made a political issue. Van Buren, who was a widower, showed his loyalty to Jackson. He went out of his way to be nice to Peggy. He hosted dinner parties in her honor, which made Jackson like him all the more.

But as the issue dragged on, slipping from secrecy into the nation's press, Van Buren realized it was weakening the party. Finally, in 1831, he figured a way out.

He induced Eaton to resign from the Cabinet and resigned himself. The other Cabinet members were forced
to do the same, including the Calhoun men whom Jackson wanted to get rid of. It left the president a free hand
to form a new cabinet of loyal followers. What had
started as a social dispute ended in great political change.

The mass resignations of the Cabinet caused a national sensation. A government turned upside down? It
had never happened before. But the stubborn and self-
righteous Jackson would not give an inch. He even
charged that the scorning of Peggy Eaton was a plot
cooked up by the wicked Calhoun and his followers. It
was quite like the president to say that evil enemies
were to blame for the scandal. Many thought the president had come close to making a fool of himself.

The Eaton Affair is an example of how personality
can shape political decisions. Petty and subjective feelings and motives can influence the behavior of powerful
people like Jackson and turn a whole country in this
direction or that, more by accident than by design.

Through one of those famous Washington "leaks,"
Jackson acquired another grievance against his vice
president. Back in 1818, Jackson learned, Calhoun had
privately tried, in Monroe's Cabinet, to have Jackson
censured for his invasion of Florida. No question now
that Van Buren was the president's choice for his successor.

The feud between Jackson and Calhoun became even
hotter when Calhoun led South Carolina in its opposition
to a high protective tariff. The South had expected Jackson to support their position. He didn't because it would
have lost him the support of important Northern states.
The Congress did revise the tariff in 1830, but only with
trifling changes. That enraged Calhoun's South Carolina
followers. They became the most radical states' rights
advocates in the entire South. If heavy duties on English
imports continued, they feared it might cripple the

planters who sold cotton to the English textile mills. Calhoun argued that the cotton culture was the under-pinning of slavery. So a high tariff was not only a threat to prosperity but a threat to slavery.

Calhoun was well aware that the North outnumbered the South two to one in population. By majority rule, then, it could pass whatever tariff it wanted. To over-come that handicap, Calhoun developed the theory of nullification, that is, the right of a state to protect itself from "the despotism of the majority." Through a state convention, he wrote, a state could declare null and void an act of the national government.

The threat of nullification didn't scare Jackson. And it only mystified many who couldn't figure out the fine legal points of Calhoun's argument. Wasn't "nullification" just a fancy word for "treason"?

In a famous debate with Senator Robert Y. Hayne of South Carolina, Senator Daniel Webster denounced nul-lification as a false doctrine that would destroy national unity. The federal government, he said, in his rich and deep voice, is the expression of the will of the people, not of the states. The national interest is greater, much greater, than that of any state or section. It is not a question of Liberty first, and Union afterwards, he con-cluded, but "Liberty *and* Union, now and forever, one and inseparable!"

Soon after the debate, the nullification advocates arranged an elaborate dinner on April 13, 1830, to honor Jackson's birthday. The real motive was to glorify states' rights and win broader support for their movement. Many toasts were offered to that effect, and then the president was asked to offer one. Jackson stood, held up his glass, and with strong emphasis said, "Our Federal Union. It must be preserved." Dead silence fell over the company. Calhoun's hand shook so much that the wine spilled down the side of his glass. He knew Jackson had declared war against him.

*Daniel Webster speaking to the Senate in the great debate
with Robert Hayne over states' rights and nullification.*

Calhoun's followers continued to mutter threats of
preventing the collection of the tariff within the state's
borders. Then in 1832, Congress adopted a compromise
bill to reduce the tariff moderately. That didn't satisfy
the nullifiers. In control of the South Carolina legislature
for the first time, they passed a resolution declaring the
tariff null and void and banning the enforcement of it

within the state's boundaries after February 1, 1833. But the nullifiers had strong opposition within the state. They met in convention as the Unionists and declared themselves ready to support the federal government. It looked like civil war might break out in South Carolina.

Jackson was furious at the challenge. He thought Calhoun must be going crazy. South Carolina was threatening rebellion, and he would have liked to hang those nullifiers for treason. But he controlled his rage and tried to use both carrot and stick to get over the crisis.

He issued a proclamation to the people of South Carolina, warning them in a fatherly tone that their politicians were trying to destroy the Union. (Considered Jackson's most important state paper, the proclamation was written by his secretary of state, Edward Livingston.) At the same time, Jackson had Congress pass a Force Bill to allow him to send troops into the state to enforce the law.

Calhoun decided he had to give a little himself. He didn't like the split between the two South Carolina factions. He teamed up with Henry Clay to work out a bill that reduced the tariff on many items. With that compromise on the table, South Carolina repealed its nullification law. (The day happened to be the president's sixty-sixth birthday.) So the crisis was over, and both sides claimed victory.

It gave Jackson no lasting pleasure. He predicted that the nullifiers would one day "blow up a storm on the slave question. . . . This ought to be met, for be assured these men would do any act to destroy this union and form a southern confederacy. . . ."

Whatever his motives, Jackson had acted decisively to maintain the Union against the worst threat it had yet faced. In contrast, he supported the state of Georgia when it defied an important ruling of the U.S. Supreme Court.

12

INDIAN
REMOVAL
★

When Jackson came to power, white settlers were still trying to take over large areas of land the Indians clung to. There were now some 65,000 Indians living in the Southeast. Called the "Five Civilized Tribes" by the whites, they included Cherokees, Creeks, Choctaws, Chickasaws, and the Seminole. They were the largest Indian concentrations within the states of the Union.

These Southeastern tribes were farmers as well as hunters. For the last two or three generations, they had given their labor to the soil. White traders, government agents, and missionaries had encouraged them to fence their farms, use the plow, and raise cotton and corn for the market. Hundreds of Protestant missionaries had worked among them for almost twenty years, educating the children in the agricultural, mechanical, and household arts. They aimed to make the Indians literate and Christian. And the government encouraged the work by providing special funds.

By the mid-1820s, many Indian leaders had built up valuable plantations, mills, and trading posts. The Cherokees and Choctaws especially were proud of the progress they had made in adapting themselves to the white man's culture. But this did not lessen their love for their homeland. They wanted to enjoy their new way of life here on what was left of their ancestral grounds.

Against their determination to resist pressure to move was the whites' resolve to take their increasingly valuable land for cotton planting and mining. (Gold had been discovered in Cherokee territory in 1828.)

Jackson's election reinforced the whites' desire to relocate the tribes west of the Mississippi. The president wanted the Indians cleared out of the path of his white civilization. The old argument that the farmer had a superior right to the land over the hunter sounded plausible to many whites so long as the tribes involved were "savage." But here was the Cherokee nation, which had embraced plantation agriculture (and slavery), devised its own alphabet, and established a constitution, schools, newspapers, and churches. How could these people be removed? Had not President John Quincy Adams himself said that *cultivated* Indian lands would *always* be respected?

The damned Cherokees! said the angry whites. Those Indians had turned to civilized ways for the perverse purpose of confounding the white men who wanted to get rid of them. The whole trouble with the Cherokees, Calhoun had told a Cabinet meeting, was precisely their progress in civilization.

It was embarrassing. But people have always been able to find a reason to justify their desires. The whites came up with a new ground for expelling the Cherokees. The Indians had no right to alter their condition and become farmers! The governor of Georgia, where many of the Cherokees lived, said that yes, God wanted Georgian soil to be tilled, but by the *white* man, not the Indians.

Just as the Cherokees were realizing the goal of white civilization that so many had advocated for them, the American government was abandoning it, and them.

In Jackson's first message to Congress, he took up the Indian question:

The people . . . of every state . . . submit to you the interesting question whether something cannot be done, consistently with the rights of the States, to preserve this much-injured race [Indians]. . . . I suggest, for your consideration, the propriety of setting apart an ample district west of the Mississippi, and without the limits of any State or Territory now formed, to be guaranteed to the Indian tribes as long as they shall occupy it. . . .

There they may be secured in the enjoyment of governments of their own choice subject to no other control from the United States than such as may be necessary to preserve peace on the frontier and between the several tribes. . . . This emigration should be voluntary, for it would be as cruel as unjust to compel the aborigines to abandon the graves of their fathers and seek a home in a distant land. But they should be as distinctly informed that, if they remain within the limits of the States, they must be subject to their law.

What was Jackson saying? That the Indians can no longer exist as independent nations within the states. They must either go west or become subject to the laws of the states.

Sure of the president's backing, four Southern states moved against the Indians. They passed bills nullifying the legal force of Indian customs. Heavy penalties were levied against any Indian who might enact or enforce tribal law. And punishment was threatened for those who would interfere with or discourage Indian emigration.

The crisis soon came to a head in Georgia. The legislature declared the Cherokee tribal council illegal. Its laws had no effect in Cherokee territory. It was Georgia that had full control over both the tribe and its lands. Soon after, the Cherokee were forbidden to defend their interests by bringing suits against whites in the state's courts, or even by testifying in such cases. It meant a claim brought by a white against an Indian—no matter how fraudulent—could not legally be protested.

What protection was left to the Indians? The state had taken away all their legal rights. The Indians protested to Washington.

Jackson was blunt: You have no hope of relief from the federal government, he said. If you don't like it, move.

The Cherokees took their plea for recognition as a self-governing people to the U.S. Supreme Court. They won their case in 1832, in *Worcester* v. *Georgia*. With a fiery denunciation of the wrongs committed by the state of Georgia upon the Indians, Chief Justice Marshall held that Georgia had no right to extend its law over Cherokee territory. It was contrary to solemn treaty rights and to the Constitution. The Cherokee were jubilant.

But victory in the highest court did not protect the Indians. Georgia, with the president's blessing, defied the court ruling. The state knew it could count on the old Indian fighter. One of the first pieces of business for Jackson's new administration was passage of the Indian Removal bill. It provoked a fierce debate in Congress. Senator Theodore Frelinghuysen of New Jersey took the floor to argue that the Indians had a superior title to the land:

> *I believe, Sir, it is not now seriously denied that the Indians are men, endowed with kindred faculties and powers with ourselves; that they have a place in human sympathy, and are justly entitled to a share in the common bounties of a benignant Providence. And, with this conceded, I ask in what code of the law of nations, or by what process of abstract deductions, their rights have been extinguished? . . . How*

can Georgia . . . desire or attempt, and how can we quietly permit her, to invade and disturb the property, rights, and liberty of the Indians? . . . How can we tamely suffer these States to make laws, not only not founded in justice and humanity "for preventing wrongs being done to the Indians" but for the avowed purpose of inflicting the gross and wanton injustice of breaking up their government, of abrogating their long-cherished customs, and of annihilating their existence as a distinct people?

I proceed to a discussion of those principles which . . . sustain the claims of the Indians to all their political and civil rights as by them asserted. And here I insist that, by immemorial possession, as the original tenants of the soil, they hold a title beyond and superior to the British Crown and her colonies and to all adverse pretensions of our confederation and subsequent Union. . . . No argument can shake the political maxim that where the Indian has always been, he enjoys an absolute right still to be, in the free exercise of his own modes of thought, government, and conduct. . . .

The confiding Indian listened to our professions of friendship; we called him brother, and he believed us. . . . We have crowded the tribes upon a few miserable acres on our Southern frontier: it is all that is left to them of their once boundless forests; and still, like the horse-leech, our insatiated cupidity cries, give! give! Do the obligations of justice change with the color of the skin?

A new concern for human rights was emerging, especially in New England and the Northeast. Freedom for the black slave, reform of prisons, improvement of treatment for the mentally ill, temperance, public education, the rights of women, and now justice for the Native American were causes that began to draw passionate support. Petitions signed by thousands flooded into Congress to protest the Indian Removal bill. Speeches, editorials, and articles were reprinted in pamphlet form to rally popular support.

What about treaties with the Indians? people asked. Didn't they recognize Indian sovereignty and Indian rights?

Georgia's Governor George G. Gilmer had a ready answer:

> *Treaties were expedients by which ignorant, intractable and savage people were induced without bloodshed to yield up what civilized people had a right to possess by virtue of that command of the Creator delivered to man upon his formation—to be fruitful, multiply, and replenish the earth, and subdue it.*

Gilmer was saying that treaties were merely tricks to get without force—or often after applying overwhelming force—what the "civilized" white man wanted from the "savage" Indian.

"Is it one of the prerogatives of the white man," asked Senator Frelinghuysen, "that he may disregard the dictates of moral principles, when an Indian shall be concerned?"

It seemed that it was.

Jackson had his way. The Indian Removal Act of 1830 was adopted by Congress in a close vote. Robert Remini, Jackson's biographer, wrote that "it spelled the doom of the American Indian. It was harsh, arrogant, racist—and inevitable. It was too late to acknowledge any rights for the Indians. They had long since been abrogated."

Under this law, the government was permitted to enter into treaties trading land in the West for Indian lands in the East. A permanent guarantee of possession of the lands was given, as well as compensation for improvements already made, and aid for the emigrants.

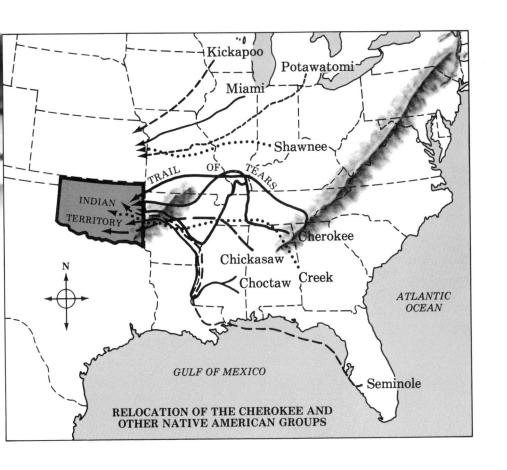

Kickapoo
Potawatomi
Miami
Shawnee
TRAIL OF TEARS
INDIAN
TERRITORY
Cherokee
Chickasaw
Choctaw
Creek
N
ATLANTIC
OCEAN
GULF OF MEXICO
Seminole

**RELOCATION OF THE CHEROKEE AND
OTHER NATIVE AMERICAN GROUPS**

The law authorized removal *only if the Indians gave consent.* But anyone who knew Jackson's history, and the history of the frontier, understood that the use of force would be inevitable.

Congress put up only half a million dollars to compensate the Indians for the loss of lands and the expense of moving the five tribes and getting them settled west of the Mississippi—in "Indian territory," in what is now Oklahoma.

About 23,000 Choctaws and some Cherokees were pressured into moving during 1831–32. Others refused to go and were forced out: the Alabama Creeks in 1836, the Chickasaws in 1837. "Through the use of hypocrisy, bribes, lies, suppression of critics, and intimidation," wrote historian Edward Pessen, the Jackson and Van Buren administrations secured approval of nearly eighty treaties that were despised by most of the Indians.

The Cherokees stubbornly refused to go. Year after year they resisted in every way they could, while white speculators and Southern politicians got more and more impatient. Finally a small group of Cherokees, without authority to act for their nation, entered into a fraudulent treaty with the government, agreeing to removal. The Army moved in to enforce it. The soldiers seized 15,000 Cherokees who had refused to move at the appointed time. The Indians were forced out of their homes, separated from their possessions, and taken off to military detention camps. Kept in captivity for months, hundreds died. Men, women, and children trudged along through the winter months, hurried on their way by soldiers, so that they could not even stop to take care of the sick or bury the dead.

A fourth of the Cherokee nation died on this Trail of Tears, a forced migration that one historian has said "approached the horrors created by the Nazi handling of subjected peoples." Others have called it "one of the most disgraceful episodes in American history."

*"The Trail of Tears": the forced migration of the Cherokee
Nation to the west, painted by Robert Lindnieux.*

It helps to grasp the enormity of the crime if we sift
through what the government did in the process of removing all the Southeastern tribes, not only the Cherokees. The migration west—the largest forced
migration in American history—stretched out over several years. Although Jackson had left the White House by
the time the Cherokee exodus began, much of the blame
for the inhumanity belongs to him. The 800-mile journey
west was marked by brutality and corruption. Many
Indians did not have the proper clothing to march
through freezing Southwestern winters. If they traveled
in summer, they suffered from extreme heat and
drought. The federal government had farmed out the
removal of the tribes to private enterprise, that is, to
profit-making contractors. These people were paid

twenty dollars a head for the Indians they removed. Secretary of War Lewis Cass hired the same speculators who had cheated the Indians to do this job. In their greed for profits, they fed the Indians scanty and contaminated rations. The meat was rancid, the flour spoiled, the drinking water foul. Some of the food was years old and marked unfit to eat. The Indians were crowded onto old unseaworthy boats that caused many accidents. The worst one killed 311 Indians. The Army, as we have seen, played a major role in Indian removal. It worked with the contractors. The soldiers put thousands of Indians labeled "troublemakers" in chains and rounded up those who tried to flee.

The journey west went through territory where cholera raged. Worn down by the exhausting march, weakened by the bad food, tens of thousands of people died of disease and exposure. In the end, from one-fourth to one-third of the Southeastern Indians perished as a result of federal policy.

The more the Indians suffered and died, the more indifferent were the federal officials responsible. Government records show great attention to details of logistics, and massive indifference to the appalling effects of what the government was doing. It cannot help but remind anyone familiar with the Holocaust of the way the Nazis concentrated on the details of rounding up and shipping prisoners to the death camps, while they totally ignored the cost in human suffering.

The hypocrisy of the federal government is almost beyond belief. President Jackson always presented himself to the Indians as the "benevolent father." Right down to his Farewell Address, where he said good-hearted people "will rejoice that the remnant of this ill-fated race has at length been placed beyond the reach of injury and oppression, and that the paternal care of the General Government will hereafter watch over them and protect them."

Jackson would not recognize what his policy had done to the Indians, much less take responsibility for their destruction. Nor would General Lewis Cass, who carried out Jackson's orders. "The extinction of the Indians," he wrote, "has taken place by the unavoidable operation of natural causes. . . . Their misfortunes have been the consequence of a state of things which could not be controlled by them or us."

As the Cherokee chief John Ross said, "The perpetrator of a wrong never forgives his victims." Whites responded to the mass deaths of Indians by denying reality itself. To many Americans, Indians were "things" or "lice," less than human.

13

THE WAR AGAINST THE BANK

★

At the same time that Jackson fought his relentless war against the Indians, he fought another war—against a bank—the Bank of the United States. In the Jackson legend it is often called the war against the money power. Here is the courageous president battling for the benefit of the "little man." The climax comes when he drives the corrupt Nicholas Biddle (president of the Bank) and his money changers from the temple.

What was that war about?

We need to go back a bit to set the stage for it. It begins with Alexander Hamilton, President Washington's financial wizard. Hamilton saw that to survive, the struggling new nation needed solid finances. He believed in America's potential as an economic power and was determined to promote its growth. To that end, in 1791 Congress chartered the Bank of the United States. Partly private, partly government-financed and -controlled, it was meant to stabilize the government's finances and establish its credit.

The Bank would serve as the government's financial agent. It would collect taxes, provide a safe place to deposit the government's funds, and lend the government money when needed. Since gold and silver, the basis of all international trade, was in short supply, the Bank could issue bank notes. And by lending to new businesses, the Bank could help expand the economy.

The Bank's charter expired in 1811, but in 1816, President Madison rechartered the Bank for twenty years. This second Bank would serve the same purpose of spurring growth. But now it had the tough job of regulating the money policies of the hundreds of state banks that had recently sprung up. Men got charters from state legislatures to set up banks they expected would make large and quick profits from the boom in commercial enterprise and manufacturing. They invested as little of their own capital as possible, put out as much paper money as they could get away with, and speculated madly. They extended credit much too easily, and printed money without the backing of gold or silver in their vaults to cover their obligations. That speculative fever pushed them to the brink of failure. And when the Panic of 1819 came on, the Bank of the United States demanded they pay their obligations not with paper money but in coins of gold or silver. Many were unable to; they collapsed, bringing down the whole system of credit.

A severe depression followed, as we've seen. Wages were cut by two-thirds or more, workers were slashed from payrolls, and land sales sank to a fraction of what they had been. Businesses went bankrupt, factories folded, farms and plantations stood abandoned as prices and exports fell. Many people blamed the Bank for their troubles, accusing it, with some justice, of mismanagement and fraud. They believed no bank could be trusted, especially the big national bank.

But with the return of prosperity in the 1820s, public attacks upon the Bank almost stopped. The fact was that by 1829, its young, handsome, and energetic president, Nicholas Biddle—who began guiding the Bank in 1823— had made it into an efficient institution. Headquarters in Philadelphia and the twenty-nine branches throughout the country provided many useful financial services and played a responsible role in a period of rapid expansion.

★

Under Biddle the Bank promoted the best interests of the country, its Treasury, the state banks, and their creditors. It was able to move funds from one place to another as needed. It tried to keep state banks from making unwise loans by insisting that they back loans with gold or silver coin. And it called in its own loans when it spotted trouble. The Bank continued to take federal deposits, make commercial loans, and buy and sell government bonds.

Financial experts at the time agreed that the Bank could help prevent the economy from running wild again and collapsing. Politicians seemed to feel the same, for the Bank was not made an issue. When Jackson ran for president the first time, in 1824, he did not campaign against the Bank. Nor did he in the 1828 election, when he played down his position on all controversial issues.

So when President Jackson in his first annual message to Congress in December 1829 called for the end of the Bank, as it was then set up, he startled the country. Many Jacksonians, even some of his Cabinet, disagreed with him. They favored the Bank, as did such important nationalist politicians as Daniel Webster and Henry Clay. But Jackson insisted on forcing the issue.

He had strong personal reasons for disliking the Bank. He himself had once suffered a near disaster because of it. He had never liked banks after that, and particularly this one. Besides, his enemy Henry Clay championed the Bank, with an eye to using it as an issue to defeat Jackson in the 1832 election. Jackson charged the Bank was the beneficiary of special privilege, granted a monopoly of the government's business by charter. That monopoly, he said, hurt the common man, the people his politics played to. Not only was the Bank evil, he went on, it was also unconstitutional.

For many people the Bank was the Devil's own if their idol, Old Hickory, said it was. Others had more material reasons to hate it. Speculators in Western lands didn't want Biddle's Bank to keep tight control over state or local banks. And state bankers who needed easy credit were jealous of Biddle's power to decide who got it and who didn't.

The Bank's twenty-year charter was not due to expire until 1836. Biddle wanted to move quietly to guarantee its extension now, and he worked with his friend Clay to accomplish it. Historians agree that whatever its flaws, the Bank did serve the economy and the nation well. It gave the country the best banking system it would have until the Federal Reserve was created in 1913. Unhappily for Biddle, the born aristocrat, he was arrogant and condescending, unable to win the people's support for his case. In a democracy, that left him a loser.

It can't be said that Biddle was without blame for the attack upon the Bank. He made loans to congressmen at lower rates than others got. And he spent lots of money to buy favors from the press, hiding it by manipulating the Bank's records. He also gave sizable loans on very agreeable terms to many anti-Jackson editors in the bigger cities. On the opposite side, the state and local banks did the same thing for newspapers which attacked the Bank. It was a common practice, hardly excusable just because everybody did it.

Meanwhile, Henry Clay, who had already been nominated for president in December 1831 by a national convention of his party, decided it would serve his own presidential ambitions if he fronted for Biddle in applying for a new charter early in 1832. He reasoned that if Jackson should veto the recharter bill—and he hoped Jackson would!—it would cost Jackson enough votes in the East to put Clay into the White House.

Clay persuaded Congress to vote in favor of renewing the Bank's charter, even though it had four years still to run. In his intensely personal way, Jackson said to Van Buren, "The Bank is trying to kill me, but I will kill it."

With the help of others, he drafted a veto message meant to rally the public behind his war against the Monster Bank. It was a masterpiece of propaganda, stirring up every popular prejudice against the Bank. He said the Bank was undemocratic, unconstitutional, and—that word so often used as an appeal to patriotism—un-American. He portrayed it as a dangerous monopoly and then, in a moving passage that still applies, set forth what a democratic government should do for its citizens:

> *Distinctions in society will always exist under every just Government. Equality of talents, of education or of wealth, can not be provided by human institutions. In the full enjoyment of the gifts of heaven and the fruits of superior industry, economy, and virtue, every man is equally entitled to protection by law. But when the laws undertake to add to these natural and just advantages, artificial distinctions . . . to make the rich richer and the potent more powerful, the humble members of society, the farmers, mechanics, and laborers, who have neither the time nor the means of securing like favors to themselves, have a right to complain of the injustice of their government. Its evils exist only in its abuses. If it would confine itself to equal protection, and, as heaven does its rains, shower its favors alike on the high and the low, the rich and the poor, it would be an unqualified blessing. In the act before me, there seems to be a wide and unnecessary departure from these just principles.*

Here Jackson was posing as the people's champion against the special interests. The emotional appeal was irresistible, and Congress failed to override his veto. How do historians weigh the significance of his veto? "As a politician," writes the historian Richard B. Morris,

"Jackson had added immeasurably to the popularity and power of the Presidential office by acting as a defender of the common man against a rapacious moneyed aristocracy, but as a tamperer with finance and currency he set the banking system of the country back for a whole generation."

This nineteenth-century political cartoon depicts "General Jackson Slaying the Many-Headed Monster"—the Second Bank of the United States—symbolized by the human heads with the names of the states on them. The bank's president, Nicholas Biddle, is the large top-hatted head in the center; Jackson, armed with his veto stick, is on the left; and Major Jack Downing, a popular character invented by the humorist Seba Smith to poke fun at the president's backwoods supporters, is on the right.

Look at the broader significance of the veto for a moment. On the surface, it makes the president the legislative equal of two-thirds of the Congress. But really, in five cases out of six, he equals less than one-sixth of the Congress—the difference between the majority needed to first pass a bill and the two-thirds needed to override the veto.

As for Jackson's use of the veto, "It seems clear," writes the historian Edward Pessen, "that it was his personality rather than a reasoned philosophy that justified, in his mind, the setting aside of Congressional measures, Supreme Court rulings, or individual officeholders he, Andrew Jackson, disagreed with or disliked." He was a man with an overwhelming conviction of his own rightness.

Jackson's frequent use of the veto shows how much the power of the executive office increased during his administration. The first six presidents vetoed a total of eight bills (both Adamses and Jefferson vetoed none). Jackson vetoed twelve bills, or more than all his predecessors together. Recently President George Bush, in his four years in office, vetoed thirty-one bills.

Jackson, like a number of presidents to come, tried to separate the people from their delegates in the legislature. Those men in Congress, he said, were "hungry little bands of interest seekers . . . not the same as the whole people with a common interest." In such serious crises as the Bank War, Jackson believed the people needed to rely upon the president, the one man elected by them all, to say to the Congress, No, you cannot do this, not unless you have two-thirds to overcome my veto.

Jackson's conduct of foreign affairs was of a piece with his style in domestic matters. In his first message to Congress, he said his policy was "to ask nothing that is not clearly right, and to submit to nothing that is wrong."

*During Jackson's reelection campaign of 1832, this
Whig cartoon, "King Andrew the First," attacked him for
his frequent use of the presidential veto power.*

The people liked that. He was telling the world the rights of Americans must be respected. He was all for using practical rather than formal means to settle differences between the U.S. and other nations. But if agreement could not be reached peaceably by compromise or adjustment, he was ready to use the threat of force.

Jackson's first success was in overcoming severe British restrictions on U.S. trade with the West Indies. By compromise he also got the French and other European nations to pay U.S. claims against them for damage to American commerce and property during the Napoleonic wars. His administration was the first to work out commercial treaties between the U.S. and Far Eastern countries. Jackson acted promptly and energetically to make foreign powers realize they must treat the United States with dignity and respect.

Still, at times he could go too far in making threats; he was quick to react violently to insults, real or fancied. Once, during a dispute, he almost brought America to the brink of war with France. On the whole, however, Jackson managed to win from Europe recognition of America's status as a free and independent power, worthy of the respect accorded far older nations.

The battle over the Bank came to a head a few months before the 1832 election. Jackson's Kitchen Cabinet had decided years before that he must run again in 1832. They believed only he could win and that a second term would consolidate their party. They also wanted Van Buren to be his running mate, figuring that if the sickly president should die in office, the New Yorker would carry on his program faithfully.

The Democratic nominating convention took place in May 1832. It was called simply to put the party's stamp on Van Buren for the vice presidency. The delegates didn't even bother to nominate Jackson for president. They simply approved the nominations he had already received from the state parties. Nor did the convention adopt a platform, or ask Jackson to make a speech outlining his principles. After all, everyone knew—or thought they knew—what Jackson stood for.

Although these were the first national nominating conventions for both parties, it didn't mean they were any more democratic than the old caucus system they replaced. The small cliques of party managers controlled everything of importance, just as they always had.

The election year began badly for Jackson. He caught influenza, which can be terribly weakening for a man of his age and poor condition. And then a bullet Jesse Benton had fired into his arm twenty years before had worked its way closer to the surface and was causing great pain. A surgeon agreed to remove it. Anesthesia was unknown then, and Jackson watched his doctor cut into the bare arm and squeeze it until the ball of metal popped out. After the wound was dressed, Jackson went right back to his desk. He would not let the operation interfere with business.

How the president appeared at this time was captured by Henry Wikoff, a young man who visited Jackson one evening in the White House after a dinner party:

> *The doors were thrown open and General Jackson entered at the head of his company, talking and laughing with much animation . . . seating himself near the fire[;] his friends formed a group about him. I was absorbed for some minutes scanning the face and mien of this remarkable man. . . . He was tall, slim and straight. . . . His head was long, but narrow, and covered with thick grey hair that stood erect, as though impregnated with his defiant spirit; his brow was deeply furrowed, and his eye, even in his present mood, was one to threaten and command. His nose was prominent and indicated force. His mouth displayed firmness. His whole being conveyed an impression of energy and daring.*

★

That summer of 1832, Jackson went back to the Hermitage, leaving the campaign to his advisers in Washington and the Democratic politicians in the states. A torrent of advice and propaganda streamed out to the army of Jacksonians. The Monster Bank was made the chief issue, with Biddle painted as "Czar Nicholas," its villainous master. The liberty-loving common man was dramatized as the hero fighting off the wealthy aristocrats. Vicious charges were made against Clay, with outright lies peddled freely about his personal life.

Biddle countered by pumping large sums of money into press and pamphlet attacks upon Jackson, and the spoils system and the Eaton affair came in for heavy blows too. While Jackson *talked* about democracy and liberty, said Clay's men, he *acted* like a tyrant, scrapping the Constitution and making his will the Supreme Law.

Somehow Jackson appeared to be coated with Teflon, to use a word applied to President Ronald Reagan about 150 years later, when Reagan ran for reelection. Nothing negative about Jackson seemed to stick. People voted for him with little regard for issues. The cult of personality prevailed. Voters in Pennsylvania, for example, were known to be opposed to every stand that Jackson took on issues, yet those same voters, without hesitation, dropped their Jackson ballots into the box on election day.

When it came to issues, voters then, as now, backed local and congressional candidates who agreed with them. But issues seemed not to matter when they voted for a president. As more than one analyst has said, "The American voter at times is clearly a most unpredictable citizen."

When the returns came in, Jackson celebrated a decisive victory. He got fifty-five percent of the popular vote as against thirty-seven percent for Clay and eight percent for William Wirt, the candidate of a new third party, the Anti-Masons, made up of people who opposed the Masons and all other secret societies. The electoral college gave Jackson 219 votes, Clay 49, and Wirt 7.

As one of the major newspapers said of Jackson's victory, "The devotion to him is altogether personal, without reference to his course of policy." Perhaps it's worth noting, however, that Jackson's popular vote was somewhat under the 1828 returns—the first time that had happened in a president's reelection.

14

LIFE AT THE HERMITAGE

★

By his veto, Jackson had wounded the Bank, but he had not killed it. On the last day of his first term, the House resolved that "government deposits may . . . be safely continued in the Bank of the United States." The congressmen were reminding the president that the Bank's charter still had four years to run. It was a slap in the face; it only made the president all the more determined that the Bank must die.

The next day was Inauguration Day. This time there would be nothing like the chaos of four years ago. It was bitter cold in the capital, and snow blanketed the city. To hold the formalities outdoors was impossible. Jackson took the oath of office in the House chamber and dispensed with a reception at the White House. Feeling very old and tired, he soon went up to bed. As he turned the pages of Rachel's Bible, he thought longingly of the Hermitage and a time when his political troubles could be forgotten.

Toward the end of his first term, Jackson had begun work on plans to remodel the Hermitage. He wanted such sweeping reconstruction that it would change the whole look of the house. The two wings would be enlarged, with a library and a study added, and a dining room large enough to seat a hundred guests. A two-story portico held up by tall, slender Doric columns would give the south front the elegant appearance befitting the mansion of a large slaveholder.

Jackson's court painter, Ralph Earl, did this portrait of the General astride his horse, Sam Patch. There are thirty-four known portraits of Jackson done by Earl.

When alterations to the Hermitage were finished, the president ordered expensive furniture from Philadelphia to fit it out in high style. He placed his adopted son, Andrew Jr., now twenty-one, in formal charge of the plantation. In his own hand, the president prepared a brief manual on how to run a plantation and sent it to Andrew Jr. with some words of advice for a young man always running into debt:

> *You will have to begin to learn the wants of a family and supply it. This will require economy and care which you will have to attend to if you expect to get through life well by always knowing your means and living within them. . . . Write me fully as to the situation of all things—the health condition of the Negroes, the appearance of my stock, the colts in particular. . . .*

Jackson enjoyed horse racing and betting as much as ever. He kept colts in the White House stable and entered them in nearby racetracks, but using a friend's name. Everyone knew, of course, who the owner really was. (It was considered unseemly for a president to operate a racing stable, and right from the Mansion.) As was common in that time, black jockeys rode the Jackson horses.

One year after the Hermitage was remodeled, a fire ruined it. It happened one afternoon in October 1834, fortunately while the family was not at home. Sparks from the chimney probably ignited the wooden roof, and in a high wind the flames rapidly spread. Some of the furniture was saved by the slaves, but many letters by Rachel were lost. The walls of the Hermitage survived and the mansion could be rebuilt on the same site. Andrew Jr.'s family moved to a neighbor's home while a large work crew began rebuilding the house, this time with a roof of tin. Jackson decided on several alterations

The Hermitage as it looked during the late 1840s.
A lithograph by Francis W. Strickland.

to improve the style of the house and to enlarge it so that more people could live in it comfortably.

To pay for the high cost, some Jacksonians began a subscription drive, but the president stopped that at once. He felt it was wrong for a president to accept gifts from the public. With winter coming on, he asked Andrew's wife, Sarah, and her two children—Rachel, now two, and Andrew II, about eight months—to come live with him in the White House. Andrew Jr. would join them when the Hermitage was roofed over and the cotton crop sent to market. As little Rachel came in the door, she flung herself into the president's outstretched arms and said, "Grandpa, the great fire burnt my bonnet, and the big owl tried to kill Poll [her parrot] but Papa killed the owl!"

Overburdened as he was with presidential cares, Jackson still paid close attention to the everyday details of managing the Hermitage plantation. He knew all too well how careless and lazy Andrew Jr. was, and how much he loved the bottle. Jackson peppered him with letters of caution and advice, Andrew replying—when he did!—cheerily and optimistically. He wrote Sarah too of how much he missed her and the grandchildren after they returned to Tennessee:

> *I have not rested well at night since you left me— everything appeared silent and in gloom about the House, and when I walked into your room—found it without its occupants—everything changed, the cradle of my little pet without it, and its little wagon there—my feelings were overcome for the moment. . . . I wish I could see her walk, and hear her begin to prattle. . . .*

But the absence of Sarah's babies was made up in part by the presence of Emily Donelson's children in the White House. Her eldest (another Andrew!) was six as the second term began. He had his own pony and rode out with the president now and then. Mary Rachel was three, and another baby was born in May. When the children came down with the measles, the president was as anxious as Emily. If he heard a cry from the nursery, he would get up in the dark and pad through the corridor to see what was troubling his pets. In his letters to friends, he often had as much to say about the children as about politics. And when the children were away, he worried that they might forget him. Sometimes their noisy play upset him, but if they were gone, he complained he was lonely.

More often, however, he was surrounded by babies and young children—not only his own grandchildren and the Donelson children, but others whose families brought them. The holidays were celebrated with both adults and children invited. One Christmas festival, for instance, began at 4 P.M. with a frolic in the East Room. Blindman's buff, puss in the corner, and forfeits were played before supper, and then the children had a snowball fight—with cotton balls—indoors. After supper they stood in line by the door to bow or curtsey to the president as they left.

Meals in the Red Room were usually a joyous time with young men and women—the children of friends, and staff officers of the military or the diplomatic corps— crowding the tables, eating, laughing, courting. A typical informal dinner given weekly at the White House was described by John Montgomery, a Pennsylvania lawyer, in town for a Supreme Court appeal. He wrote his daughter that about twenty people sat down to dinner at 6:30:

The table was very splendidly laid and illuminated. There was a large chandelier hanging over the middle of it with 32 candles besides those on the table, mantles and on the piers. The first course was soup in the French style; then beef bouille, next wild turkey boned and dressed with brains; after that fish; then chicken cold and dressed white, interlaid with slices of tongue and garnished with dressed salad; then canvasback ducks and celery; afterwards partridges with sweetbreads and last, pheasants and old Virginia ham. The dishes were placed in succession on the table, so as to give full effect to the appearance and then removed and carved on a side table by the servants. The first dessert was jelly and small tarts in the Turkish style, then blanc mode and kisses with dried fruits in them. Then preserves of various kinds; after them ice cream and lastly grapes and oranges.

The wines on the table were sherry and port to drink with soups and the first course of meats. When the wild turkey and fish were served, Madeira was handed and while the wild fowl was eaten, champagne was constantly poured by the servants; after these were gone through with, claret was put on to drink with the fruits. As soon as all had taken what their appetites could possibly endure, we left the table and returned to the drawing room. . . . Soon after . . . a cup of coffee was handed, then the ladies played the piano and sang and after this a glass of liqueur was sent around as the signal for adjournment and the party broke up about half past nine o'clock.

With all this fine dining, the White House was not without its annoyances. Once, returning from a trip, the president wrote ahead to a White House staffer to make sure the place was rid of bedbugs.

As "friend of the common man," open to all, the president held frequent mass receptions and expanded the usual dinners and levees enormously. In his mind, the White House belonged to the people; anyone at whatever hour could enter the mansion to see the president and shake his hand. No guards stood at the gate. Knock at the door, a porter would admit you, and a servant would lead you into a parlor. The president would interrupt what he was doing, greet you and chat for a few minutes.

Unlike Washington or Jefferson, Jackson was not a theatergoer. But he welcomed touring companies to the White House, as he did dancers, singers, and artists, treating them warmly and respectfully. His own preferred White House entertainment was the musicale.

When his health permitted, Jackson took horseback rides daily, and also went out for an afternoon walk with

Ralph Earl. But as his condition worsened, he kept more to home, often staying all day at his desk. He got up early and went right to work. He seemed driven by the need to do his duty. His correspondence—with officials, politicians, friends, family, citizens—had him penning ten to twenty letters a day. Some of them ran to eight or ten pages of handwriting. Jackson performed his work calmly and precisely, "in utter defiance of bodily anguish," as one of his secretaries said, and even when "he was suffering the acutest pain and when he was so pitiably feeble that signing his name threw him into a perspiration."

The president moved about freely, with no armed guards to protect him. Neither he nor anyone else feared for his safety. But on May 6, 1833, only two months after his second inaugural, an ominous incident occurred. With some of his Cabinet, Jackson was headed by steamboat for Fredericksburg, Virginia, where the president would lay the cornerstone for a monument to George Washington's mother. Sitting in his cabin as the ship lay at dock, he was reading a newspaper when the door burst open and a man came in. It was Robert B. Randolph, a former navy lieutenant who had been dismissed for theft on Jackson's order. Randolph suddenly slapped Jackson in the face. The president tried to rise and grapple with him but was wedged between a table and the bunk. Friends of Randolph who had come aboard with him seized him and rushed him off the boat.

Much later Randolph was brought to trial for criminal assault. Jackson, recalling his pledge to his mother never to indict any man for striking him or for suing him for slander, would not testify at a trial that took place long after he left office. He even asked his successor, President Van Buren, to pardon the man if found guilty and to remit any fine. That, he said, "might have a good effect upon society."

This was the first time in the forty-year history of the young republic that a president had been attacked. It was by no means the last, for attempts to kill presidents would become an appalling fact of life. Only two years after the Randolph assault, on January 30, 1835, as Jackson was leaving the funeral of a congressman in the House chamber, a man stepped up to him with a small concealed pistol and fired it directly at the president's heart from a distance of only eight feet. Instead of ducking, Jackson lunged at the man with his cane. The man dropped the pistol and fired a second gun, held ready in his other hand, at the president. Another explosion thundered out. And again Jackson started forward at the gunman. The young man turned to flee but was knocked down by a Navy officer.

The assassination of President Jackson was attempted in 1835 by Richard Lawrence. This lithograph by an unidentified artist was quickly circulated in an era before television allowed the public to see such major events immediately.

What had happened? Although the caps of both pistols had discharged, they failed to ignite the powder in the barrel, perhaps because a thick mist had dampened everything. Jackson was hurried to a carriage and driven to the White House. Vice President Van Buren, who followed shortly, was astonished to find the president sitting with one of the Donelson children in his lap and chatting quietly with General Scott.

The gunman turned out to be an unemployed housepainter named Richard Lawrence. Immediately brought to trial for an attempt at assassination, it became clear he fantasized wildly, blaming Jackson for standing between him and his "rightful" claim to the throne of England. Lawrence was found not guilty by reason of insanity, and committed to an asylum.

Jackson immediately gave the attack political significance. He was convinced it had been plotted against him by his enemies, though no evidence to prove it ever came to light. Some attributed Lawrence's deed to Jackson's own personality, saying he was so powerful, so dominating a character, that he invited the attention of lunatics. Others said no, that social conditions in the United States had become so oppressive for a great many people that an assassination attempt was but one symptom of something terribly wrong.

15

A TIDE OF
REFORM

★

A month after the first attack upon him, the president began an extensive tour of New England. He expected his parade through the towns and cities would set off demonstrations of patriotic fervor and awaken national pride. Only Washington and Monroe had traveled the country before now. Neither, however, had caused the emotional explosion the sight of Jackson would ignite.

On June 6, 1833, the presidential party left the White House and set off for Baltimore. For the first time, Jackson rode in a railroad train, the newfangled technological marvel. A huge crowd greeted him on his arrival in Baltimore. By coincidence, the Indian leader Black Hawk came to the city the same day, sent by the government on a tour of the eastern states so that he would see the power of America and the futility of resisting removal of his people beyond the Mississippi. Black Hawk was brought to the president's hotel to hear a grim warning from old Sharp Knife: if Black Hawk ever took up arms again, he would be severely punished. That evening both men went to the theater, where the audience ignored the play to stare at the president and the first Indian most of them had ever seen.

On the way from Baltimore to Philadelphia, Jackson rode under a banner stretched across the road which read, THE UNION—IT MUST BE PRESERVED! A carriage drawn by four white horses brought the president to his hotel as 30,000 people cheered his passage through the city streets. There was a reception for invited guests at Independence Hall, but a mob forced its way in, eager to shake the General's hand. Then came a military parade, lasting five hours, with Jackson sitting upright in the saddle to take the salutes. Exhausted as he was, that night he attended a military ball.

The next day the party went by steamboat to New York. As Jackson landed at Castle Garden, 100,000 people roared a welcome from housetops, wharves, ships, and streets. The president mounted a horse and led a parade up Broadway to City Hall Park, the people jamming both sides of the street. The governor presided over the welcoming ceremony, and the weary president headed for a hotel to rest.

"The Grand Triumphal Tour," they called it, as the president headed for New England—New Haven, Hartford, Pawtucket, Dorchester, and then Boston. Jackson was utterly worn out but determined to go on. In Boston he began to hemorrhage; a doctor came to his hotel, bled him once, then again, and finally let him rest. Feeling a bit stronger two days later, Jackson was determined to go through with the ceremony at Harvard University, which was conferring on him an honorary degree of Doctor of Law.

John Quincy Adams, the former president and one of Harvard's board of overseers, objected strongly. He could not bear to witness Harvard's "disgrace in conferring her highest literary honors upon a barbarian who could not write a sentence of grammar and hardly could spell his own name." Neither charge was true of Jackson, but Adams hated him so much he could not stand silent. Harvard's president, Josiah Quincy, replied to Adams that "As the people have twice decided this man knows enough law to be their ruler, it is not for Harvard College to maintain that they are mistaken."

After accepting the degree, Jackson began to shake

the hands of all the undergraduates and the faculty as they filed past. Finally, he was driven off to Charlestown, where he climbed the unfinished Bunker Hill Monument and sat through an oration by the long-winded Edward Everett. Another series of receptions followed, and then on to Lynn for a dinner in his honor. Then Marblehead, Salem, and Lowell. When a severe hemorrhage tore through his lungs, it appeared this would end the tour, but Jackson said no, I owe it to the people expecting to see me; let's finish it. At Concord, New Hampshire, the tour did end when the president collapsed. Stops in Maine, Vermont, and upstate New York were canceled. A steamer carried the president back to Washington, where, in the White House, his life seemed to ebb away. For forty-eight hours Vice President Van Buren stood by, ready to take the oath of office. But once more, Jackson recovered and went back to work.

When Jackson visited Lowell, Massachusetts, on his tour, the textile mills were closed to free the workers to celebrate the president's arrival. He asked to have them reopened so he could see how the mills operated. The president was amazed by the complex degree of industrial organization that neither he nor most Americans were yet familiar with. Lowell was a new town, built as a model community, with immense factories and workers' housing. Some 5,000 young women, all under thirty, made up seventy percent of the work force. They came to Lowell from the countryside, the first women to labor outside their homes in large numbers. The mill owners recruited unmarried women eager for economic independence and to enjoy freedom away from the isolation of the farm. Once married—and most of them did marry—they left the factory forever. The mills set a twelve-hour day, six days a week, and paid about three dollars a week. (Better pay than domestic servants, who got seventy-five cents a week, or seamstresses, paid ninety cents.)

*"Lowell Girls," depicted on a bank note, at work
in the Massachusetts textile center.*

Jackson asked the workers dozens of questions. He watched them carding, spinning, and weaving at the long rows of machines. Man-made canals brought water from the rushing rivers to generate the water power that drove over 200,000 spindles. It was regimented labor, and exhausting. Sexual discrimination didn't make it easier. It was built into the factory system, with men getting the better jobs and better pay. Nor was sexual harassment unknown, for foremen and other male workers took advantage of their power.

A year after the president's visit, hard times hit Lowell. Prices fell, sales were off, inventories mounted. The managers ordered a fifteen percent wage cut, to protect their profits at the expense of the workers. The women struck briefly, but failed to prevent the pay cut. Soon hours were lengthened, work loads increased, and production speeded up as the owners tried to maintain their profits. The women at Lowell and in other mill towns protested, and in one place formed a union.

The situation in Lowell illustrated how industrialism had begun to take root. But America was still a nation of farms and small towns. In 1830 the population of the nation was 13 million. Only one of fifteen citizens lived in cities of over 8,000. Most production was still carried out not in huge complexes like Lowell but in small shops. The typical American expected to become a capitalist. For any hardworking, ambitious person, enterprise was a kind of religion. The Jacksonian goal was to enlarge opportunities for such individuals, without imposing government limits.

It was during Jackson's era that trade unions sprang up in most of the nation's cities. Skilled and semiskilled workers formed separate journeymen's societies. Printer, blacksmith, saddler, carpenter, baker, tailor, mechanic, weaver, rope and sail makers—they and people in scores of other trades saw the need to unite for higher wages, shorter hours, and an end to speedup. While many of their leaders were workmen, other men with reputations as reformers and friends of labor were accepted as leaders too.

The unions were among the first to embrace other social reforms. They wanted to abolish imprisonment for debt (in 1830, five out of every six people in the jails of the Northern states were debtors, most of them owing less than twenty dollars), to reform land laws, to expand schooling for the poor, to extend the right to vote. . . . They believed labor's welfare was best served by bringing about significant changes in American society as well as by improving conditions in the shop.

Joining together to enlarge their treasuries and their strength, the unions turned to the strike as their principal weapon. In 1835 and 1836—the last part of Jackson's time in office—hundreds of strikes were waged throughout the country. In many places the long hours of labor that had prevailed for generations were lowered as the result of successful strikes for the ten-hour day.

The attempt by laborers to organize themselves in order to bargain collectively was resisted by the employers. Often employers turned to the government or the courts for help. The many canals being built at this time provide an example of how the Jackson administration cooperated with the corporations. The workers— often newly arrived immigrants put to backbreaking manual labor—suffered long hours and low wages. On the Chesapeake and Ohio Canal, in Maryland, the laborers had been recruited from one place, County Cork in Ireland. They organized a secret militant society to improve their working conditions and pay rates. The construction company, determined to smash the union, brought in a new group of Irish workers, from County Longford. The Cork men viewed the newcomers as threats to their own security and fought to keep them out. Early in 1834, pitched battles between hundreds on each side caused deaths and arrests. President Jackson, the self-proclaimed friend of the workingman, sent in federal troops to put down the labor troubles.

The employers could rely on the courts to start criminal prosecutions of unions on the charge of conspiracy to violate the laws of the land. In 1835 the Society of Journeymen Tailors in New York increased its rates and won acceptance after a brief strike. A few months later the employers combined to force the rates down to the original level. When the tailors struck again, the employers had twenty of their leaders indicted for criminal conspiracy. The jury convicted them, and the judge imposed heavy fines. Angered by the outcome, William Cullen Bryant, the poet who edited the *New York Evening Post*, wrote:

> *They were condemned because they had determined not to work for the wages that were offered them! Can anything be imagined more abhorrent. . . . If this is not slavery, we have forgotten its definition. Strike*

the right of associating for the sale of labor from the privileges of a freeman, and you may as well at once bind him to a master. . . . If it be not in the color of his skin, and in the poor franchise of naming his own terms in a contract for work, what advantage has the laborer of the north over the bondman of the south?

Not until 1846 would a judge of the Massachusetts Supreme Court rule that the purpose of a union was neither criminal nor carried out by criminal means.

The rise of unions was but one sign of a rich and diverse pattern of social reform that began around 1830.

Liberal ministers preached to their congregations that the rich were getting richer and the poor poorer. They attacked the evils of the new factory system that saw women and children working from dawn to dark at pitiful wages and under dreadful conditions. Didn't Christ's teaching of brotherhood apply to the bleak city slums?

Among the well-to-do there were some men and women whose hearts answered to the calls for help from those handicapped by poverty or physical or mental defects. They used their wealth liberally to support many worthy causes and charities. Government in Jackson's time did little to help people in distress; that duty was considered the concern of the rich or private groups.

Another sign of reform was the birth of many "third parties." They spoke for minorities who felt the two major political parties did little or nothing to satisfy their needs and interests. Workingmen's parties especially grew rapidly, from 1828 on, and could be found not only in the major cities but in small towns everywhere. Almost all had their own press that reported the party's activities and encouraged reform programs. These small, short-lived groups did not aim to win elections but rather to focus attention on the range of abuses that hurt mostly the nation's working people. Sometimes they cooperated with the Democrats on particular issues, while warning their followers that neither major party was concerned with the real problems of workers.

Much stronger than the worker groups was the Anti-Masonic Party. It blended religious zeal with hatred of aristocracy and fear of the secret order of Freemasons. The party grew with furious speed in rural areas of New England and the Midwest, fueled by charges that the Masons conspired to spread terrorism, anarchy, and atheism. It opposed Jackson in the 1828 and 1832 elections and was absorbed into the Whig Party after 1834. Its leadership came mostly from ambitious and opportunistic politicians who tried to ride it into power and office.

The other important political movement of Jackson's era was the Nativists, backed largely by middle-class people. They held that anyone of foreign birth was unfit for citizenship, as were all Roman Catholics, who they said owed their allegiance not to this country but to the pope. Nativists were found generally in the larger cities where the Irish newcomers settled. The Nativists feared their political strength was threatened by the flood of immigrant poor into this country.

As the tide of reform swept the nation, it brought about many important changes in American life. A passion for education created the public school systems while it extended education to adults as well. Cheaper newspapers served a widening reading public. Dedicated social reformers set out to right the many wrongs that afflicted America: treatment of the insane, of prisoners, of the aged, of women, of children.

It was all part of an optimistic, confident nationalism. People believed democracy must and could be made perfect. The best American thought grappled with the problem of how to improve human welfare.

"What is man born for," asked Ralph Waldo Emerson, "but to be a Reformer, a Remaker of what man has made, a renouncer of lies, a restorer of truth and good?"

16

ABOLITION—AND
REPRESSION

★

In 1829, a few months after Jackson entered the White House, a tall, lean, black-coated newcomer to Boston gave the Fourth of July address to a frock-coated audience in the Park Street Church. In his deep voice, young William Lloyd Garrison flung out a challenge:

> *I stand up here to obtain the liberation of two millions of wretched, degraded beings, who are pining in hopeless bondage—over whose sufferings scarcely an eye weeps, or a heart melts, or a tongue pleads either to God or man.*

Our politics is rotten to the core, he went on. All alike are guilty of the national sin of slavery. We in the free states, he continued, are constitutionally involved in the guilt of slavery. It is our duty to speak out against its continuance, and to assist in its overthrow.

His words reached only a few. But some eighteen months later, on New Year's Day, 1831, the first issue of his small four-page newspaper, the *Liberator*, appeared. Probably President Jackson paid no attention to it. But its message would reverberate like thunder in the land.

> *I will be as harsh as truth and as uncompromising as justice. On this subject, I do not wish to think, speak or write, with moderation. No! No! I am in*

*earnest—I will not equivocate—I will not excuse—I
will not retreat a single inch—AND I WILL BE
HEARD. . . .*

The campaign to abolish slavery did not begin with Garrison. As early as 1773, slaves petitioned for their freedom in Massachusetts. In 1775, Philadelphia Quakers organized an antislavery society. During the Revolutionary War, slaves fought for American independence on the promise of freedom.

Slave rebellions had begun as far back as the seventeenth century, only fifty years after the first Africans reached Jamestown. The uprisings stirred deep fear in the slaveholding communities, and the result was the adoption of many laws limiting the activities of slaves and free blacks. In 1801, when Andrew Jackson was a Tennessee judge, Gabriel Prosser of Virginia planned a large-scale insurrection in Richmond. But a great storm washed away the doomed rebellion, and Gabriel and many other blacks were hanged. In 1822, in Charleston, South Carolina, Denmark Vesey plotted one of the most extensive slave revolts ever recorded, only to be betrayed by a frightened house slave. Vesey and thirty-four others were executed.

Then in 1831, during Jackson's first term, the greatest slave revolt of all broke out. It was led by Nat Turner, a plowman and preacher. He felt he was called by God to lead "the children of Israel" out of bondage. The black rebels killed fifty-five whites in Southampton County before the revolt was crushed. Turner and many other slaves were hanged. Nowhere, now, did white slaveholders feel safe.

Those years saw ever more rigid laws controlling slaves as fear grew over the dangers the African Americans posed to the security of life, property, and the South's economic system. The criminal law became a tool for the suppression of abolitionist beliefs and ac-

★

tions. Close regulations were also imposed on free blacks and whites who might associate with and assist slaves in their search for freedom.

Southern whites became almost an army in civilian clothes, and African Americans a subject people in an occupied country under near-martial law. Schooling of blacks was forbidden, their church services and ministers closely watched, freedom of movement or assembly limited unless passes from masters were first obtained. The Southern myth of a great happy family disrupted by Northern agitators hardly conforms with the harsh reality.

When Garrison and others founded the American Anti-Slavery Society (AASS), in Philadelphia in 1833, they declared publicly what the organization stood for: immediate emancipation. But they vetoed the use of physical force as a means of gaining their ends. Moral persuasion was their method. They would do only what was lawful in serving their cause.

At first, Garrison's had been a small voice crying in the wilderness. Communications were primitive and costly; it took money and great skill to make yourself heard. But the rapid growth of industry and technology made travel and communications cheap and quick. By the early 1830s, the abolitionists were able to build a network of well-coordinated pressure groups. And when a few rich and influential white merchants, like the Tappan brothers of New York, joined the antislavery movement, their money enabled the abolitionists to take full advantage of the revolution in printing. Steam-powered presses cut the cost of printing so much that the abolitionists could flood the country not only with newspapers and pamphlets but with kerchiefs, primers, hornbooks, etchings, woodcuts, emblems, and even candy wrappers bearing the antislavery message.

Taking advantage of the cheap postal rates, the abolitionists mailed out hundreds of thousands of free papers

THE LIBERATOR.

VOL. I.]   WILLIAM LLOYD GARRISON AND ISAAC KNAPP, PUBLISHERS.   [NO. 33.

BOSTON, MASSACHUSETTS.]   OUR COUNTRY IS THE WORLD—OUR COUNTRYMEN ARE MANKIND.   [SATURDAY, AUGUST 13, 1831.

Above: The masthead of William Lloyd Garrison's antislavery newspaper, issue of August 13, 1831. Right: A poster put up in Boston on October 21, 1835, calling for a violent attack upon the British abolitionist George Thompson, known to be visiting Garrison's newspaper office on that day.

THOMPSON,
THE ABOLITIONIST.

That infamous foreign scoundrel THOMPSON, will hold forth *this afternoon*, at the Liberator Office, No. 48, Washington Street. The present is a fair opportunity for the friends of the Union to *snake Thompson out!* It will be a contest between the Abolitionists and the friends of the Union. A purse of $100 has been raised by a number of patriotic citizens to reward the individual who shall first lay violent hands on Thompson, so that he may be brought to the tar kettle before dark. Friends of the Union, be vigilant!

Boston, Wednesday, 12 o'clock.

to all parts of the country, aiming especially at influential people. In July 1835 their propaganda reached Southern ports. The South was enraged by this invasion of their territory. Overnight, the right of free speech and free press became an extremely hot issue.

President Jackson found himself in the thick of it. We know what his view of slavery was. Raised in a slave-dependent society, he had become a large slaveholder himself, buying African Americans, selling them, punishing them if they tried to run away to freedom, betting them on horse races, offering them as gifts . . . so when he defined "democracy," he never said anything about slavery. His party felt it had no need to defend slavery, for the slave system was no concern of government.

Didn't people have a right to their private property—and that included slaves—without interference from the federal government? That right was basic to the idea of freedom in Jackson's mind. To pass laws abolishing slavery was unthinkable—it would undermine the very foundation of American government, the president believed.

High-sounding theory, yes. But no wonder Jackson would not entertain attacks on a system that served his personal needs so well. This was a golden age for such great planters as Old Hickory. Year after year, the cotton harvest increased enormously, and so did the profits it brought.

In supporting slavery, Jackson's party was not alone. It was a time when politicians of both parties abused blacks. But his rival, the Whig Party, never united on the race question, although a few of its leaders sympathized with blacks. The Whigs were far more united on hating the Irish and the Roman Catholic Church. Generally, the Jacksonians were the party of those same people—the Irish immigrants. The Democrats led racist drives that stripped free blacks of the vote in several Northern states. When it came to race baiting, Jackson's followers were outstripped by no one. No other issue but race confronted the nation with such terrible dilemmas— moral, psychological, economic, political. Jackson saw abolitionism as "the vexing question, the dangerous rock to our Union."

One way to avoid that danger, he thought, was to rid the country of those slaves who had been freed or were born free. He became one of the officers of the American Colonization Society, formed in 1817 to establish a colony for free blacks in West Africa. Other officers included Madison, Monroe, Clay, and Calhoun, all slaveholders like Jackson. They considered free blacks to be a "menace." They persuaded Congress to buy some territory in Africa, named Liberia (after the word "liberty") and called its capital Monrovia (after President

Monroe). At its outset, free blacks and white abolition-ists opposed it as an "outrage" formed for the benefit of slaveholders who simply wanted to get rid of free blacks at public expense and increase the market value of their own slaves. Only about 15,000 blacks, including many emancipated slaves, were actually transported to Li-beria.

Whites could be so inconsistent and hypocritical on this issue. The society's leaders said they wanted to send free blacks to Africa to improve their lot, but they fought against any attempt to expand their political rights here at home. (Improve their condition, and they would want to stay!) African Americans were accused of being shiftless and incompetent, and then were hated when they proved not to be. Accused of being ignorant and stupid, but denied education. Accused of being immoral, but forced to become the mistresses of the same slave-holders who declared themselves to be insulted and degraded if placed next to a black person in a public place. With all the lip service white Americans paid to equality, they in fact practiced every form of inequality when it came to African Americans and Native Ameri-cans.

Bigotry, supplemented by cruelty and greed, under-lay the atrocities committed against both peoples. So too did bigotry incite violence against those whites who joined with blacks in the fight for freedom and equality. In New York City, for example, during the Jackson years there were frequent clashes between the abolitionists and the proslavery elements—mostly gangs of Irish ma-nipulated by the rulers of Tammany Hall, the Democratic stronghold. On July 7, 1834, a mob attacked a church on Chatham Street where a black congregation was wor-shiping. Several people were injured, and the interior of the church wrecked. Two nights later, another mob set out to catch Arthur Tappan, president of the AASS, and hang him. On their way to his home, they stopped at the

house of his brother Lewis, an equally ardent abolitionist, but he had been warned by a watchman who raced
ahead of the mob and had fled with his family. The rioters
smashed into the undefended house, wrecked the interior, piled the furniture on the street, and set it afire.

Two days later, several hundred men converged
upon Arthur Tappan's silk store on Pearl Street and
stoned the building. When police tried to stop them,
several officers were stabbed and beaten badly. The
rioters sacked and burned a dozen houses and a black
church. Several black people caught on the street were
captured and mutilated. Only the arrival of the National
Guard halted the carnage. That evening the rioting broke
out again, with more churches destroyed. It took de-
tachments of infantry and cavalry to bring it to a bloody
end.

So many antiabolition riots broke out the next year—
1835—that it became known as the "Mob Year." The
Southern press hurled cries of "fanatic," "traitor," "cut-
throat," "foreign agitators," and "infidel" at Garrison and
his followers, cries echoed in the Democratic papers of
the North. "These dangerous men agitate a question
that must not be tampered with," said one Boston paper.
"They are plotting the destruction of our government,
and they must not be allowed to screen themselves from
the enormity of their guilt." A New York paper carried a
letter from a prominent South Carolinian insisting that
abolitionists be "silenced in but one way—*Terror-
Death.*"

Abolition agents were mobbed everywhere. In Nashville, Tennessee, young Amos Dresser, a vendor of
Bibles from an Ohio seminary, was charged with being
an abolitionist and whipped by a mob in the public square.
In one week, over a hundred press reports appeared
describing mob violence. Meetings were broken up by
force. That fall the *Niles Register*, a Washington newspaper of great importance, noted some 500 recent inci-

dents of mob violence. "Society seems everywhere un-hinged," wrote the editor, "and the demons of 'blood and slaughter' let loose upon us. The character of our coun-try seems suddenly changed."

There was continued and ample evidence for that fearful observation. In July a ferocious antiblack riot broke out in Philadelphia when a black servant struck his employer. Two white abolitionists were lynched in Mis-sissippi for promoting an alleged slave insurrection plot. And on the night of July 29, the leading citizens of Charleston, South Carolina, broke into their post office and grabbed stacks of abolitionist literature just arrived by mail packet from New York. The next night, 3,000 people gathered around a huge bonfire to watch Charles-ton "purify by fire" the abolition pamphlets and to hang Garrison in effigy.

State officials endorsed the deed. And Amos Ken-dall, Jackson's old crony, now promoted to postmaster general, refused to interfere. Even though seizing the mail is illegal, he said, any postmaster refusing to deliver "inflammatory papers would stand justified before the country and all mankind." Jackson fully agreed with Ken-dall in this policy, calling abolitionist literature "a wicked plan of inciting the negroes to insurrection and massa-cre." Kendall informed the postmaster in New York City, from where the abolitionist mail was being sent, that he could exclude antislavery material from the mail. Thus the Jackson administration stymied the postal cam-paign at its point of origin—in direct violation of the Bill of Rights and federal law.

Southern states not only suppressed abolitionist pro-paganda; they asserted the obligation of the Northern states to suppress any activities within their borders "disturbing to the peace and security" of their sister states in the South. That December of 1835, in his annual message, President Jackson reacted to the aboli-tionists' postal campaign. He denounced the organized

*Defenders of free speech used this lithograph
in 1835 to protest First Amendment violations
by proslavery forces, including President Jackson.
It shows a mob in Charleston, South Carolina,
breaking into the post office to seize abolitionist
literature and burn it.*

antislavery movement as "incendiaries" and called for
"severe penalties" to suppress their "unconstitutional
and wicked" activities. He praised the Northerners who
mobbed antislavery speakers, broke up abolitionist
meetings, and destroyed antislavery presses. He called
upon postmasters to publish the names of every person
who subscribed to antislavery papers, and for a national
censorship law to stop such men as Arthur Tappan from

sending incendiary literature through the mails into the South.

Since Jackson's administration had already taken extralegal steps to deny the abolitionists the mails, such a law would be merely a legal nicety. Throughout the South, state politicians had dug up old ordinances or devised new ones to stop the circulation of abolitionist material.

Surprisingly, at first glance, John C. Calhoun and his states' rights supporters were about as angry over Jackson's proposal of federal censorship as were the Northern abolitionists. Calhoun believed each Southern state, *not* the federal government, should use its own authority to decide what papers were "incendiary" and to ban them from the mails. If *Congress* asserted that right, then a Northern majority might vote to let antislavery papers flood the South. And beyond, it would mean all barriers the slave states had built "for the protection of their lives and property" could be torn down by acts of Congress. Finally, wouldn't Jackson's proposal really grant Congress "the power to abolish slavery"?

In the end, no law was passed. Northern politicians simply closed their eyes to the South's violations of law and free speech. They knew it would go on anyhow. Jackson's successors adopted the same hardheaded view. Amos Kendall's censorship policy prevailed right up to the Civil War.

How someone from outside saw such events as these was put with great clarity by Alexis de Tocqueville, a French aristocrat who visited the United States and published his impressions in *Democracy in America* in 1835. This passage goes behind what happened in Charleston, and the White House response to it:

> *I know of no country in which there is so little independence of mind and real freedom of discussion as in America. . . . In America, the majority raises*

formidable barriers around the liberty of opinion; within these barriers, an author may write what he pleases; but woe to him if he goes beyond them. . . . He is exposed to continued obloquy and persecution. His political career is closed forever . . . every sort of compensation, even that of celebrity, is refused him. . . . He is loudly censured by his opponents, whilst those who think like him, without having the courage to speak out, abandon him in silence. He yields at length, overcome by the daily effort which he has to make, and subsides into silence, as if he felt remorse for having spoken the truth. . . .

17

"IS IT BLOOD SHED FOR PLUNDER?"

★

Violent mobs could brutally choke off freedom of speech, but what about the Congress of the United States? Surely the makers of federal law would defend the First Amendment to the Constitution, even if President Jackson did not?

The test soon came when the House of Representatives faced a flood of abolitionist petitions. Remember: the right of the people "to petition the government for a redress of grievances" is a basic part of the First Amendment. It guarantees the means to dissent or protest.

Yet when a congressman from Maine in December 1835 presented a petition praying for the abolition of slavery in the nation's capital, a Virginian quickly moved that the petition be laid on the table. And the House agreed to it by a big majority. Two days later, a South Carolinian demanded that such petitions be rejected "peremptorily," without a hearing. A New York congressman called that totally unacceptable. To reject a petition outright, without even a hearing, was to deny the sacred right of petition. But that didn't matter to Southerners. They made it clear the abolitionists had to be stopped, regardless of the law and the Constitution. There is but one way to deal with "fanaticism," said one Southerner, and that is to "strangle it in its infancy."

For the next five months, former president John Quincy Adams, now a representative from Massachusetts, protested that to restrict free speech in the Congress was a "direct violation of the Constitution of the United States, of the rules of the House, and of the rights of my constituents." Again and again he took the floor to deliver passionate speeches against the South's position. Finally, the House voted to bar itself from printing, receiving, or even mentioning the contents of any petitions related "in any way" to the subject of slavery. Most of the Northern Whigs supported Adams in voting against it. It was the Northern Democrats who supplied the votes the South needed to pass the "gag rule," as it was called. President Jackson, his party's leader, was silent.

The gag rule didn't silence the abolitionists. Year after year they barraged Congress with their petitions, tens of thousands of them, calling for the abolition of slavery and the slave trade in the District of Columbia, for legislation barring slavery from Western territories, against the admission of any new slave state, for abolition of the interstate slave trade, and, of course, for repeal of the gag rule. By the spring of 1837, an astonishing 2 million people had signed antislavery petitions.

Since the original gag rule was a resolution, not a standing House rule, it had to be renewed at each session. And year after year, Adams—who commanded more attention than anyone else in Congress—led the fight against it. Dubbed "Old Man Eloquent" for his stubborn stand, the name stuck; he became a new folk hero.

Finally, in 1844, enough votes—108 to 80—were mustered to end the gag rule once and for all. After a nine-year battle, Adams did it by convincing the Congress that limiting free speech endangered the Union. What gained Adams a majority was the growing realization in the country that the question of slavery was identified with the right of petition, the right of free speech, the right of freedom of the press. People might not want to become abolitionists, but they would not stand by and see their freedoms taken away by slave-holders. Adams showed great courage by persisting in the struggle. Death threats, mostly from Southerners, came often in his mail, sometimes a dozen assassination letters a month. They did not intimidate him, though they frightened his family. He never thought of resigning from Congress or tempering his powerful language. If Jackson did not scare easily, neither did Adams.

You will recall that at the end of his first term, Jackson had vetoed renewal of the charter of Biddle's Bank of the United States. The charter still had four years to run, however. Jackson took his reelection to mean that he had public support behind his drive to get rid of Biddle's Bank. He decided to cripple it by removing federal deposits and distributing them among selected state banks. When some of his Cabinet disapproved, Jackson forced them to resign and appointed others favorable to his policy. The Cabinet must be a president's personal instrument, he believed. There was no room for dissent.

By the end of 1833, Jackson had chosen twenty-three state banks as depositories, defending his action by accusing the Bank of the United States of trying to influence elections. When the Senate asked to see his message to his Cabinet listing the reasons for removal of deposits, Jackson refused. Clay then had the Senate adopt a resolution censuring the president because he "has assumed upon himself authority and power not conferred by the constitution and laws, but in derogation of both." Charge and countercharge flew back and forth between the White House and the Congress. In the end, Senator Benton, now Jackson's close friend, got the Senate to erase the censure resolution from the record. Jackson had won. The Bank of the United States failed to secure a new charter from Congress. Biddle turned his operation into a state bank by obtaining a charter from Pennsylvania.

Another important issue running through (and beyond) Jackson's presidency was what to do about Texas. The huge territory, belonging to Mexico, was in the path of the nation's rapid westward expansion. Reports of rich lands, lands to be had just for the taking, lured people on. Much of the land lay on the fringes of the vast Spanish-Mexican empire. Mexico had opened the great prairies of Texas for immigration in the 1820s, attracting American settlers by generous offers of land. Although the immigrants took an oath of loyalty to Mexico, it was plain they could not or would not break with their old ties. Mexican law had banned slavery in 1829, an act the U.S. immigrants—nine-tenths of them Southerners—who had come with their slaves, did not like. The American settlers so greatly outnumbered the Mexicans that they were able to force the government to repeal the law and allow them to keep their slaves.

Meanwhile the American press was campaigning to extend the U.S. boundary to the Rio Grande—well below the Mexican border. President John Quincy Adams had tried to achieve expansion by purchase, offering Mexico $1 million for Texas. He was turned down. When Jackson came to power, the South expected him to secure Texas. The cotton planters wanted that land in order to expand slavery. Let's buy it or annex it, they said. So in 1829 President Jackson raised the offer to $5 million, but this too was declined. Jackson's agent then tried bribery, and suggested force might be used if that didn't work.

Recognizing the danger, Mexico banned further immigration from the U.S. in 1830, and cut off the colonists' economic ties with their home country. But the Americanization of Texas went on. Soon there were 35,000 Americans in Texas, ten times the number of Mexicans.

In 1833 a revolution broke out in Mexico. General Antonio López de Santa Anna took power with a military dictatorship. The reply of the American settlers was to declare independence and form their own government in Texas, with Sam Houston—one of Jackson's old friends —as head of an army. The Mexicans struck back. In February 1836 they captured the fort of the Alamo at San Antonio and massacred the defenders. Under the rallying cry of "Remember the Alamo!" the Texans mobilized to stop the advancing Mexican army. At Goliad the Texans were defeated again. Two months later, however, Houston's force beat the Mexicans and captured General Santa Anna. From that time on, Texas went its own way as the independent Lone Star Republic.

Sam Houston, elected its first president, called for annexation by the United States. Houston's demand was supported in the U.S. by many people with immense speculations in Texas land and Texas securities. Money was the reason they wanted Texas recognized. But Jackson delayed recognition because he wanted a better geographic definition of "Texas." (The Texans took the hint. They promptly claimed a bigger area than had previously been acknowledged.) Another reason for delay was that strong opposition to annexation had been aroused in the North, and there was not yet enough political strength to put through annexation. When Jackson felt the time was ripe—the day before he left office in 1837—he recognized the independence of Texas.

Later, from retirement, Jackson would use his powerful influence to urge the addition of Texas to the Union. Democrats in the North backed the Southern demand for expansion, claiming the U.S. had much to gain by taking more territory.

The abolitionists continued to oppose adding more slave territory to the South. William Ellery Channing, the eminent Boston divine, tried to make the country think through the implications of expansionist policy. In an open letter he said:

*Wars with Europe and Mexico are to be entailed on
us by the annexation of Texas. And is war the policy
by which this country is to flourish? Was it for inter-
minable conflicts that we formed our Union? Is it
blood shed for plunder, which is to consolidate our
institutions? . . . Is it by arming ourselves against
the moral sentiments of the world, that we are to
build up our national honor? Must we of the North
buckle on our armor, to fight the battles of slavery?*

Of course, it did mean war. A war with Mexico that
lasted two years, a war that nearly doubled the territory
of the United States. A war that brought closer the
showdown between proslavery and antislavery forces. A
limited, not a total, war, but an event of profound influence upon our national life. Ralph Waldo Emerson fore-
saw its significance: "The United States will conquer
Mexico," he wrote, "but it will be as the man who
swallows the arsenic which brings him down in return.
Mexico will poison us."

Although Jackson had been long out of office when
the Mexican War began, his biographer William Graham
Sumner saw Jackson's hand in it:

*The Texas intrigue and the Mexican War were full of
Jacksonian acts and principles. . . . The army and
the navy were corrupted by swagger and insubor-
dination, and by the anxiety of officers to win popularity by the methods of which Jackson had set the
example. The filibustering spirit, one law for themselves and another for everyone else, gained a popularity for which Jackson was much to blame. . . .*

In still another bloody conflict, the president's role was
even more direct. We saw earlier how Jackson forced
the Cherokee nation out of their homeland to take the
Trail of Tears to the West. Four of the five Southeastern

tribes had been lined up for the removal west. But the fifth, the Seminole, stayed where they were. Angry whites demanded to know if Jackson had forgotten those Indians. They bombarded the president with petitions to remind him to get the Seminole out of Florida. Jackson sent an agent to Florida to negotiate a removal treaty. The man brought back a treaty signed by several Seminole chiefs. But even Thomas McKenney, for years the superintendent of Indian Affairs, called the treaty an open fraud, "a foul blot upon the escutcheon of the nation." Apparently it was signed upon the threat of overwhelming force. Still another treaty was produced, again the product of force and fraud used against an ever-weaker people.

Early in 1835, during a bitter winter that killed the Seminole's cattle and cut off their food supplies, General Wiley Thompson, charged with the task of getting the Seminole to leave Florida, met with 150 of their leaders. He read them this letter from President Jackson, the Great White Father himself:

My Children—

I am sorry to have heard that you have been listening to bad counsel. You know me, and you know that I would not deceive, nor advise you to do anything that was unjust or injurious. Open your ears and attend to what I shall now say to you. They are the words of a friend, and the words of truth.

The white people are settling around you. The game has disappeared from your country. Your people are poor and hungry. All this you have perceived for some time. . . .

My Children, I have never deceived nor will I ever deceive any of the red people. Even if you had a right to stay, how could you live where you now are?

You have sold all your country. You have not a piece as large as a blanket to sit down upon. What is to support yourselves, your women, and children? The tract you have ceded will soon be surveyed and sold, and immediately afterwards will be occupied by a white population. You will soon be in a state of starvation. You will commit depredations upon the property of our citizens. You will be resisted, punished, perhaps killed.

Now is it not better peaceably to remove to a fine, fertile country, occupied by your own kindred, and where you can raise all the necessaries of life, and where game is yet abundant? The annuities payable to you, and the other stipulations made in your favor, will make your situation comfortable, and will enable you to increase and improve. If, therefore, you had a right to stay where you now are, still every true friend would advise you to remove. But you have no right to stay, and you must go. I am very desirous that you should go peaceably and voluntarily. You shall be comfortably taken care of, and kindly treated on the road, and when you arrive in your new country, provisions will be issued to you for a year, so that you can have ample time to provide for your future support.

But lest some of your rash young men should forcibly oppose your arrangements for removal, I have ordered a large military force to be sent among you. I have directed the commanding officer, and likewise the agent, your friend, General Thompson, that every reasonable indulgence be held out to you. But I have also directed that one third of your people, as provided for in the treaty, be removed during the present season. If you listen to the voice of friendship and truth, you will go quietly and voluntarily. But should you listen to the bad birds that are always flying about you, and refuse to move, I have then

A cartoon satirizing President Jackson's portrayal of himself as "The Great White Father" of the Indians.

directed the commanding officer to remove you by force. This will be done. I pray the Great Spirit, therefore, to incline you to do what is right.

Washington, February 16, 1835
Your Friend,
A. Jackson

Osceola, the militant leader of the Seminole, was not taken in by the president's combination of promise and threat. He refused to sign a treaty. Legend has it that instead of taking up the pen offered him, he drew out his hunting knife and plunged it into the treaty paper, pinning it to the table. "This," he said, "is the only treaty I make with whites."

That fall of 1835 the Second Seminole War began. Bands of red and black warriors joined together to fight the United States Army. Blacks took part in all the major actions for a long time, until the black leaders were killed or captured. The remaining blacks began to feel the Seminole War was doomed. When they were captured, they were told, become our guides in the Florida swamps you know so well or we'll hang you. Most chose to live and therefore led the white troops into the deepest retreats of the Seminole.

Nevertheless, the war went on, becoming a guerrilla fight on the part of the Indians, who avoided head-on clashes with the Army. As the years passed, the war became ever more unpopular. Arms had failed to defeat the Seminole, and all offers made at peace talks had failed to break their resistance. Then the army decided on total war—to grind the Indians down by relentlessly destroying their crops, their shelters, and their sources of supplies. Osceola was captured by treachery, and died in prison. Other leaders who replaced him were also taken prisoner by betrayal or double-dealing.

In 1842, exhausted to the point of death, the Seminole gave in. Four thousand Seminole survivors were finally driven into exile by a mighty nation that boasted of its justice, its honor, its love of liberty. For seven years, Jackson and the presidents who followed him carried on a reign of terror in Florida, spending $40 million using the greater part of the armed forces, wasting the lives of 1,500 regular troops and an inestimable number of militia and civilians. The suffering of the Indians and blacks through the years of persecution, the lives lost, the property stolen, the friends and families separated—they cannot be measured.

By 1850 the policy of Indian removal had been accomplished. Only a few small enclaves of Indians were left in the eastern part of the United States that many Indian nations had occupied before the whites came. With the use of its armed power, the federal government had forced the Native Americans into a life of poverty and despair.

Near the close of Jackson's second term, Ralph Earl painted this full-length, life-sized portrait of the president. The artist considered this his masterpiece.

18

THE LAST YEARS

★

Jackson came to the end of his presidency with his popularity still intact. "General Jackson may be President for life if he wishes," one opponent admitted. In his two terms in office he showed that a president had the power to do more than simply carry out policies laid down by Congress. He could—if he had Jackson's will and energy—make government policy and change that policy as he liked. If he got the people to support him, what could the opposition do? Only call him names; the political cartoonists had soon dubbed Jackson "King Andrew the First."

One means Jackson used to assert his power and extend it far beyond even his own lifetime was to take great care that justices he appointed to the Supreme Court echoed his views. Of the seven who sat on the bench in his day, Jackson picked five. The effect was obvious. Almost any decision his Court handed down read like a campaign speech the president might have made. His judges, as one critic said, tailored decisions that would be "politically expedient, rather than legally sound."

Jackson's most important choice was to make Roger B. Taney the chief justice of the Supreme Court. It was Taney, some twenty years later, who wrote the infamous decision in the case of Dred Scott, the Missouri slave who claimed his freedom because of temporary residence on free soil. Taney held that Scott was not a citizen, that no free black had ever been one. Blacks, he went on, were "so far inferior that they had no rights which the white man was bound to respect." Going further, he ruled that the Missouri Compromise of 1820 was unconstitutional because "Congress had no power to abolish or prevent slavery in any of the territories." His words denied all hope of justice for African Americans.

To follow him into the White House, Jackson had long ago tied Martin Van Buren, his favorite adviser, to his leash. The Whigs—the new name the National Republicans had chosen for themselves—did not offer one candidate in the 1836 election, but let three favorite sons from different regions make the race. Van Buren won easily. Jackson could quit office feeling confident his Democrats would still be running the country.

As Inaugural Day approached, the White House was stripped of all the things that Jackson had acquired, including many gifts. It cost him $2,000 to have the immense load crated and shipped to the Hermitage. On his last day in office, Jackson toasted the Texas Republic, which, he said, should open the way for America to master all the lands to the shore of the Pacific.

The next day came clear and mild. Jackson left the White House for the last time and, seated next to Van Buren, rode to the Capitol cheered by thousands lining Pennsylvania Avenue. After Chief Justice Taney administered the oath of office and the new president delivered his inaugural address, the ex-president slowly walked down the broad steps to his carriage. A mighty shout burst from the huge crowd. General Jackson took off his hat and bowed.

The next day, Jackson chatted with a few old cronies about his life in office. He thought getting rid of the Bank was his greatest service. Asked if he had any regrets, he said, yes, two. He had failed to shoot Henry Clay and to hang John C. Calhoun.

The following morning, Jackson began the long journey home. With him went an Army doctor, on orders from President Van Buren to watch over the old man's failing health until he reached the Hermitage. The carriage took Jackson to the railroad station, rolling down streets nearly as crowded as on Inauguration Day. Jackson boarded the train and stood on the rear platform, his hat off, facing the crowd. They watched silently as the whistle blew and the train began to move. He bowed to them, and was gone.

Now in his seventieth year, Jackson was weak and constantly in pain. At several stops along the way home, he was greeted by thousands who came to see "the greatest man of the age," as one reporter said. In Nashville, the last stop, the General broke down and cried at the warmth of the town's welcome home. Safe again at the Hermitage, he wrote Van Buren that "the approbation I have received from the people on my return on the close of my official life has been very gratifying to me. I have been everywhere cheered by my numerous democratic republican friends, and many of the repenting Whigs with a hearty welcome. . . . This is truly the patriot's reward, and a source of great gratification to me, and will be my solace to the grave."

In the years he had been away, the Hermitage had been under the management of his adopted son, Andrew Jackson, Jr. Andrew had made a terrible mess of Jackson's affairs. A poor businessman, an easy victim of predatory "friends," lazy, weak, a heavy drinker, a womanizer, he had piled up debts his father despaired of repaying. No matter how often the old man reprimanded, warned, or advised the younger one, Andrew never listened or learned. The General himself was in poor shape to take command. His hearing was almost gone, his right eye nearly useless, his memory failing. Yet his will was as powerful as ever; he still tried to act like a warrior chief.

Just after he left the White House, the Panic of 1837 began. Was Jackson at least partly to blame? When he refused to recharter the Bank, he killed a major barrier to inflation by the state banks. Controls on speculation became even looser. Fraud and mismanagement were widespread. Paper money fell in value everywhere, banks collapsed, planters plunged deeply into debt. Prices of essential foods soared out of reach of the poor.

The ravages of the deep depression of 1837 were blamed on the policies of the Jackson administration in this lithograph by Henry R. Robinson, a Whig printmaker. The dissolution of the family, unemployment, alcoholism, poverty, are a few of the ills depicted in the illustration, while above it all shines Jackson's beaver hat, spectacles, and clay pipe.

The price of prime slaves dropped from $1,400 to $500. Speculators and borrowers went broke. To keep off his debtors, Jackson sold 840 acres of land in West Tennessee. The terrible effects were felt by all classes. But the "unsuspecting farmers and mechanics" suffered the most. The depression made about one-third of the working people jobless for long periods in the early 1840s.

All along, Jackson had declared that the state banks were better and safer custodians of the public revenue. History taught him better. Lacking any central control, the state banks were caught up in the speculative fever. Some of them falsified their books to conceal their troubles. When the depression came on, many people blamed it on Andrew Jackson's financial policies. The America Jackson had turned over to Van Buren as a "happy and prosperous" nation slid rapidly into the pit.

So did Jackson's physical condition. He hemorrhaged often and suffered crippling headaches and a steady pain in his side. His doctors bled him again and again, causing massive losses of blood that only made his condition worse. Perhaps seeking some comfort, he joined the Presbyterian Church in 1838, the church his wife and mother had belonged to. He had resisted Rachel's urging to do it much earlier because he felt a public avowal of religion would be taken as hypocritical. From now on, however, he attended services regularly, read the Bible each day, and read prayers to his family and the household slaves each evening.

That year Jackson lost his constant companion, Ralph Earl. The itinerant painter had dropped in at the Hermitage seventeen years before, and had found a home by the side of the General.

As the 1840 election drew near, Jackson tried to use his influence to shape the outcome. He kept in close touch with his friends in the capital, offering advice to the president, to his Cabinet members, to Congressmen, and to newspaper editors. His messages rallied everyone to support the Democratic program and warned of disaster should the Whigs be allowed to win.

But Jackson's hopes were disappointed. A decade of great social change had ended in a major depression. No issue seemed as important to the American people as the economic one. In the election campaign, the Whigs "out-Jacksoned the Jacksonians" by copying their formula for success—torchlight parades, barbecues, songs, cartoons, slogans, and cider. They invented a symbol for their candidate, General William Henry Harrison, who had defeated Tecumseh thirty years before. They portrayed Harrison as a backwoods Indian fighter who lived in a log cabin and, by contrast, ridiculed Van Buren as an aristocratic dandy. (Harrison's home was a mansion, not a log cabin.) No one knew what this coonskin candidate stood for, and the Whigs made him even less objectionable by framing no platform. To the voters, Harrison seemed to have all the virtues of General Jackson, and they overwhelmed Van Buren in the largest turnout in American history. More than eighty percent of the eligible voters went to the polls, giving the Whigs a fifty-three percent majority over the Democrats' forty-seven percent. The electoral majority was even greater: 234 to 60.

To Jackson, the defeat was devastating. He immediately blamed the loss on "corruption, bribery and fraud." Not only did the Whigs take states in every part of the Union, including his own, but they also captured Congress. The Whigs were in the saddle now, and the old man feared they would ride roughshod over all his programs.

That year, the Hero of New Orleans found consolation in celebrating the twenty-fifth anniversary of his great victory there. When his steamboat docked at New Orleans, 30,000 people screamed "Jackson! Jackson! Jackson!" as he stepped ashore. His carriage moved through the streets to a great demonstration of affection and gratitude. Exhausted by the journey, he was unable to attend all the ceremonies planned. On his last evening, at the St. Charles Theater, an audience of 2,000 sang "Hail Columbia" in his honor. His one regret was that the nation failed to make the anniversary of the victory a national holiday.

A month after Harrison became president, he died of pneumonia. He was the first president to die in office. Vice President John Tyler succeeded to the presidency. A Virginian, an old states' rights man, and a former Democrat, he vetoed so many Whig bills that he was angrily read out of the party as a betrayer of its principles—to Jackson's great delight. Tyler was a man he could count on to fulfill his old hope of seeing Texas come into the Union. And, as we've noted, in February 1845, just before leaving office, Tyler secured the passage of a resolution in both houses of Congress admitting Texas into the Union. Slavery's advocates had won again.

Tyler had taken advantage of the results of the presidential election a few months earlier. James K. Polk, a Democrat of Jackson's state, Tennessee, had been elected president by a narrow margin, defeating the Whig's candidate, Henry Clay. Polk had campaigned for immediate annexation of Texas, and Tyler declared it a popular mandate to incorporate Texas into the Union.

Called "Young Hickory" because he was as obstinate and partisan and convinced of his own rightness as Jackson, Polk would usurp the constitutional powers of Congress in order to drive the nation into war with Mexico. A war that Ulysses S. Grant declared was the most disgraceful war the country ever fought—a cynical land grab from a neighbor too weak to defend herself.

At seventy-five, the General was fading rapidly. He was beset by chills and fevers, he could barely write, and his conversation rambled into odd corners. When an artist asked to paint his portrait, he replied, "No more. I am too old and infirm." He could not afford a secretary, and stopped answering letters. The best he could do was to scribble a brief note in the margins, indicating what he would have said if he had been able.

Great stacks of his papers had piled up high during the past fifty years. What to do with them? A young man came in to help sort them and to take notes on Jackson's recollections of the past. The old man decided to leave his papers in Frank Blair's hands. In the fall of 1842, Jackson drew up a will. He was to be buried next to Rachel in the Hermitage garden. His debts were to be paid out of his estate. He left the Hermitage to his adopted son, who was named as executor. His slaves too were bequeathed to Andrew, except for two boys he gave to his grandson and four female slaves left to Andrew's wife, Sarah. He freed none of the 161 slaves he owned—not even his old body servant, George. Did it ever occur to him?

In his last months, Jackson was visited by many old friends, anxious to see him before he died. One of his visitors was Isaac Hill, a Jacksonian newspaper editor. "If he were another man," Hill said, "I could scarcely believe he would live a week." Jackson himself said, "I look like a blubber of water." He sat all day in an easy chair, unable to stand or walk, his Bible and hymn book beside him. As soon as the mail came, he reached for the Washington newspapers and any letter with the capital's postmark. Politics was still his strongest passion. He let President Polk know which office seekers he should appoint, from Cabinet to copying clerk.

One day John Catron dropped by. He was a Nashville lawyer Jackson had appointed to the Supreme Court. Catron much admired Jackson's flair for immediate action. "He would have blown up a palace to stop a fire," Catron said, "with as little misgiving as another would have torn down a board shed. In a moment he would

*This 1845 photograph of the dying Jackson was taken
only six years after photography was invented in France.
The famous Matthew Brady claimed he had gotten into
Jackson's home to take the picture himself.*

have willed it proper and in ten minutes the thing would have been done. He cared not a rush for anything behind: he looked ahead."

Everyone agreed that what Jackson wanted to do he did, regardless of the consequences. An apocryphal story has it that someone asked one of Jackson's slaves whether his master would get into heaven on Judgment Day. "If General Jackson takes it into his head to get into heaven," he answered, "who's going to keep him out?"

In May, unable to lie down, Jackson began sleeping propped up in bed. Now the swelling of his body from the massive edema reached his face. Visitors kept coming—thirty in one day alone—for a last look at the old man. On Sunday, June 1, he asked his family to invite his minister to visit after services to give him Holy Communion. This will be my last Sabbath, he said. But a few days later he rallied, and wrote to a New Orleans merchant ordering supplies for his Mississippi plantation—on credit, for he was some $27,000 in debt. Late that night, as Sarah watched beside him, she heard him muttering a prayer, and then the words of a hymn:

> *When through the deep waters I call thee to go*
> *The rivers of woe shall not then overflow.*

Waking at midnight, Jackson said to Sarah, "I wish to be buried without display or pomp—or unnecessary expense." The next day, he insisted on writing to Polk, offering his last bit of political advice. He lived a while longer in great pain. Then, on Sunday, June 8, 1845, at six in the evening, Andrew Jackson died. He was seventy-eight years old.

A NOTE ON
SOURCES
★

To get the flavor of Jackson himself, I found his letters to be best. Unfortunately, work on collecting them from many scattered archives and editing them began late. Thus far, three volumes of *The Papers of Andrew Jackson*, edited by Harold D. Moser and others, have been published by the University of Tennessee Press. The most recent appeared in 1991; it takes him up to 1815, thirty years before his death. The editors expect full publication will run to about sixteen volumes.

Many letters of Jackson contained in various archives are quoted in books about him, and I have made use of them. He kept no journal and wrote no memoir.

The most comprehensive recent biography is a three-volume work by Robert V. Remini, *Andrew Jackson and the American Empire, 1767–1821*, Harper, 1977; *Andrew Jackson and the Course of American Freedom, 1822–1832*, Harper, 1981; and *Andrew Jackson and the Course of American Democracy, 1833–1845*, Harper, 1984. A one-volume abridgment, *The Life of Andrew Jackson*, was published in a Penguin paperback in 1988. The author is an enthusiastic supporter of his subject.

The Life of Andrew Jackson, by Marquis James, Bobbs-Merrill, 1938, is a richly detailed and readable biography of some thousand pages, but quite uncritical. All biographers draw upon James Parton's *Life of Andrew*

Jackson, 3 vols., New York, 1861, which was prepared much closer to Jackson's time and contains valuable recollections by some of Jackson's contemporaries. William Graham Sumner in his *Andrew Jackson*, Houghton Mifflin, 1891, is a blunt and provocative critic of Jackson's personality and politics.

One of the most influential studies, *The Age of Jackson*, Little, Brown, 1945, was written by Arthur Schlesinger, Jr., before he was thirty. His book revived great interest in the era, for it contained many judgments scholars disputed and besides, was beautifully written.

Since Schlesinger's study many scholars have continued to draw their own portraits of the Jackson period. The most useful, to me, was Edward Pessen's *Jacksonian America, Society, Personality, and Politics*, Dorsey, 1969. It is a critical synthesis of modern scholarship and earlier insights, not a simple narrative of events. It goes beneath the surface to illuminate almost every aspect of the life of that time. Most valuable for anyone starting out in this field is Pessen's forty-page bibliographical essay.

Other Jackson studies I made use of include Fred Otto Gatell, *The Jacksonians and the Money Power, 1829–1840*, Rand McNally, 1967; Richard Hofstadter, "Andrew Jackson and the Rise of Liberal Capitalism," in *The American Political Tradition*, Knopf, 1948; Marvin Meyers, *The Jacksonian Persuasion: Politics and Belief*, Stanford, 1960; Douglas T. Miller, *Then Was the Future: The North in the Age of Jackson*, Knopf, 1973; Edwin C. Rozwenc, ed., *Ideology and Power in the Age of Jackson*, Anchor, 1964; and Glyndon G. Van Deusen, *The Jacksonian Era, 1828–1848*, Harper, 1959.

There are a large number of titles dealing with Jackson's Indian policy. Among those I relied on: Gloria Jahoda, *The Trail of Tears*, Holt, 1975; Francis Paul Prucha, *American Indian Policy in the Formative Years, 1790–1834*, University of Nebraska, 1970; M. Rogin,

Fathers and Children: Andrew Jackson and the Subjugation of the American Indian, Knopf, 1975; Bernard W. Sheehan, *Seeds of Extinction: Jacksonian Philanthropy and the American Indian*, Norton, 1973; and Earl Shorris, *The Death of the Great Spirit: An Elegy for the American Indian*, Simon and Schuster, 1971.

The studies of slavery and abolition in the Jackson era are even more numerous. I made particular use of Leonard L. Richards, *Gentlemen of Property and Standing: Anti-Abolition Mobs in Jacksonian America*, Oxford, 1970; Lewis Perry and M. Fellman, eds., *Antislavery Reconsidered*, Louisiana, 1979; Lawrence Goodheart, *Abolitionist, Actuary, Theist: Elizur Wright and the Reform Impulse*, Kent State, 1990; and Alice Felt Tyler, *Freedom's Ferment*, Minnesota, 1944.

A rich source of eyewitness accounts of life in that time is found in the books by European visitors who flooded these shores to see what the new nation was like. The best known are by such figures as Charles Dickens, Alexis de Tocqueville, Harriet Martineau, and Frances Trollope, but there are scores of others whose insights enlarge our understanding.

Interested readers can find a huge amount of material on such aspects of Jackson's time as the reform and labor movements, the lives of rich and poor, on farmers and agriculture, the factories and labor, immigration and city life, religion and the family, literature and the arts, commerce and banking, local, state, and national politics, foreign affairs.

Finally, there are outstanding biographies of both major and minor figures linked to Jackson: John Quincy Adams, Calhoun, Clay, Webster, Benton, Houston, Taney, Van Buren.

INDEX

ABOUT THE AUTHOR

★

Milton Meltzer, distinguished biographer and historian, is the author of more than eighty books for young people and adults. Born in Worcester, Massachusetts, and educated at Columbia University, he has written or edited for newspapers, magazines, books, radio, television, and films.

Among the many honors for his books are five nominations for the National Book Award, as well as the Christopher, Jane Addams, Carter G. Woodson, Jefferson Cup, Washington Book Guild, Olive Branch, and Golden Kite awards. Many of his books have been chosen for the honor lists of the American Library Association, the National Council of Teachers of English, the National Council for the Social Studies, and *The New York Times*.

The Jackson life is the latest of nineteen biographies, which include such subjects as Thomas Jefferson, Christopher Columbus, George Washington, Benjamin Franklin, Mark Twain, Langston Hughes, Mary McLeod Bethune, and Dorothea Lange.

Milton Meltzer and his wife, Hildy, live in New York City. They have two daughters, Jane and Amy, and two grandsons, Benjamin and Zachary. Mr. Meltzer is a member of the Authors Guild, PEN American Center, and the Organization of American Historians.